ENDORSEMENTS FOR
BRIDGING THE DIVIDE

"An honest, frank, and penetrating dialogue betw̄e
ers in the Evangelical/Mormon discussions abo
and Greg model how to have profitable conversa
ing to distinctly differing faith commitments. This
between Mormons and Evangelicals seeks to deepen und̄a   gs
while clarifying the distinctive faith statements of both. In this penetrating book, Bob and Greg model how two dramatically different
religious leaders can dialogue frankly while maintaining respect for
each other and their belief systems."

Dr. G. Craig Williford
President, Denver Seminary

"It sometimes happens when two people have become so alienated
from each other that they can't even discuss their differences anymore, that suddenly one of the parties takes a deep breath and says
pleadingly to the other, "Can we talk about it?" This is what has been
happening in recent years between some Mormons and some Evangelicals. And Bob Millet and Greg Johnson have led the way in showing us how to do it—how to talk about differences that are of eternal
importance without shouting at each other. May this marvelous book
encourage many others to join that important conversation!"

Dr. Richard Mouw
President, Fuller Seminary

"What Bob Millet and Greg Johnson have learned to do – become
friends, socialize together, ask and answer questions, and have long
and productive conversations – provides a model for how to create
greater peace in this troubled world. How needed for people of various faith traditions to synergistically address many of life's serious
issues. Enormously enlightening."

Dr. Stephen R. Covey
Author, *The 7 Habits of Highly Effective People* and *The 8th Habit:*
From Effectiveness to Greatness

"The engaging dialogue between Greg Johnson and Bob Millet over
the relationship between the Evangelical and Latter-day Saint positions on key topics is enormously helpful. Although I don't think a
divide has yet been bridged, I feel like I now know where the bridge

should be built and through this conversation may have even had a glimpse at the blue print. A must read for thoughtful people in both communities."

Dr. Craig J. Hazen
Professor of Comparative Religion and Apologetics;
Director, Graduate Program in Christian Apologetics,
Biola University

"The authors are to be commended for attempting to build a bridge over sometimes troubled waters. This is important reading for all who care about issues of interfaith dialogue. The authors demonstrate heartfelt comprehension of their respective positions on matters of eternal significance. They convey those views with clarity and under-standing. There are those who may not like or accept the message of this book. Many others, hopefully, will conclude: the world needs more such books."

Dr. Ronald Enroth
Professor of Sociology, Westmont College

"At once challenging and reconfirming, these interfaith dialogues both celebrate the majesty of Jesus Christ and push for deeper personal ac-ceptance of doctrines and practices often only culturally understood. Where distrust and animosity have frequently deafened Mormons and evangelicals from hearing the testimonies of faith in each other, this book invites all who claim devotion to Christ to consider anew His call to, 'Love one another as I have loved you.'"

Dr. Camille Fronk Olson
Associate Professor of Ancient Scripture,
Brigham Young University

"Some say we should not acknowledge truth in other religions or churches lest we compromise our Christian faith; others say that there cannot be truth and falsehood at the same time in a religion; still others say we have no obligation to be courteous or friendly toward those with whom we differ theologically. Millet and Johnson are wise enough to demonstrate that none of these things are so. Instead, they show respect for one another and each other's communities by explor-ing the points of deepest difference, without retreating from their own different commitments. This is a fine introduction to Mormon-Evan-gelical differences."

Dr. Gerald R. McDermott
Professor of Religion, Roanoke College

"Divides between peoples are bridged best by friendships in which thoughts and feelings are freely expressed For the remarkable model Bob and Greg give us, I am grateful."

Dr. Bill Heersink
Professor of Theology and Intercultural Studies,
Salt Lake Theological Seminary

"In a day and age when Christian faith and morals are being sorely tested and often discarded, now more than ever before professing Christians of all faiths need to reach out and understand one another. In their continuing dialogue in which they explore the profound theological differences between Mormons and Evangelicals while noting their commonalities and similarities, Professor Robert Millet of Brigham Young University and Rev. Gregory Johnson have contributed much over the past few years to fostering a spirit of improved understanding and mutual cooperation. Surrendering nothing of their own unique beliefs while acquiring much in the way of true Christian understanding and friendship, Bob and Greg have traveled North America speaking dozens of times to large audiences of Latter-day Saints and Evangelicals. They continue to demonstrate that respectful dialogue leads not only to better understanding and appreciation, but also to a mutual resolve to stem the tide against a growing secularism in modern Western society. This book, *Bridging the Divide*, is a model of how fruitful discussion can take place which neither Latter-day Saints nor Evangelicals need fear."

Dr. Richard Bennett
Professor, Church History and Doctrine,
Brigham Young University

"There is an excitement building in Utah regarding the state of affairs between evangelical Christians and our Latter-day Saint friends and neighbors. For years the apologetic grenades have been lobbed between both camps—often causing deep wounds and bitter, distasteful divisiveness. Pastor Greg Johnson and Dr. Robert Millet demonstrate that there is another approach. I have heard it called 'convicted civility' and it offers a refreshing model for building bridges of understanding that will inevitably become a highway for Truth."

Pastor Bill Young
Lead Pastor, The Rock Churches, Salt Lake City, Utah

"Greg and Bob do an excellent job at dialoguing about the similarities and differences between evangelical Christians and Mormons and serve as a model of how to communicate more effectively with persons who have theological differences. They approach doctrinal discussions with love and civility, while at the same time maintaining a deep commitment to their own faith."

Pastor Chris Lagerlof
Evangelism and Care Pastor, Mariners Church,
Newport Beach, CA

"Civility, generosity, and real understanding are typically the first casualties in our sound-bite religious world. Johnson and Millet take the less-traveled path and show, again, that genuine progress in interreligious dialogue remains elusive until relationships of trust and love buttress the conversation."

Dr. Spencer Fluhman
Department of Church History & Doctrine,
Brigham Young University

"We are at a time in history where the open assault on Christianity suggests or even perhaps demands that Christians, whatever our particular denomination or personal expression of the faith, will do well to focus on what we have in common and not on what divides us. The Robert Millet/Greg Johnson dialogues are heroic in their candor, integrity and courage to broach old barriers of misinformation and misunderstanding."

Kieth Merrill
President of Audience Alliance Motion Picture Studios,
Filmmaker

"The on-going dialogue between Greg Johnson and Bob Millett has been a groundbreaking approach to Mormon and Evangelical interaction. I have found this approach to be both informative and refreshing. In an age where rhetoric is often confrontational and demeaning, this dialogue demonstrates well the Christian principles of love and respect given as our guide in the Scriptures... *Let your conversation be gracious and effective.* Col. 4:6 (NLT) Knowing both Greg and Bob, I highly recommend this book as a bridge to understanding how to develop Christ-honoring relationships between Mormons and Evangelicals."

Pastor Jim Ayers
Senior Pastor, Valley Assembly of God, Salt Lake City, Utah

"Four years running, we have hosted the Millet-Johnson Conversation in the Boise area, two nights each time. It's unique and bar-raising for both Mormons and Evangelicals. Greg and Bob have modeled how to move to higher ground in our relationships with those we have significant disagreement with. They have exhibited grace to one another while they move toward a shared understanding of truth, or at least understanding where the other stands and why. They're honest about their challenges, suspicions, surprise discoveries, and have discovered the place of proper expectations. What they are on the platform is what they are in private: Curious, caring, good-humored, not defensive, and genuinely enjoying the journey. I've spent many hours with them behind the scenes and there is no doubt that there is a genuine brotherly love, one for the other. We learn from Bob and Greg that when we are 'dialed-in' relationally, we remove static and increase the possibility for clarity of truth while conversing on complex truth issues. It's my observation that they have distinctively represented their faith perspectives, but this is still difficult for some to accept. That aside, the way they have represented their views—the tone, the avoidance of angry and fearful flight and fight patterns, by itself is worthy of our attention and reflection. It's a healthy and liberating model to build on as Mormons and Evangelicals continue in the hard work of dialogue and persuasion. I highly recommend this book as 1) a model of convicted civility for anyone, and 2) a conversation prompt for Mormons and traditional Christians."

Jon Strain, Search Ministry
Boise, Idaho

"Misunderstanding, misrepresentation and ensuing acrimony have long characterized the unfolding saga of Latter-day Saint and Evangelical interactions. In this latest chapter, Greg Johnson and Robert Millet are taking the story in a radically different direction, modeling mutual respect, seeking and speaking the truth about each other, and a relationship grounded in love. If and when this turn becomes the ongoing story's principal context, look for a truly Christian ending."

Dr. David L. Paulsen
Professor of Philosophy
Brigham Young University

BRIDGING THE DIVIDE

BRIDGING
THE
DIVIDE

The Continuing Conversation
Between a Mormon
and an Evangelical

Dr. Robert L. Millet
Rev. Gregory C. V. Johnson

MONKFISH BOOK PUBLISHING COMPANY
RHINEBECK, NEW YORK

Printed in The United States of America.

Library of Congress Cataloging-in-Publication Data

Millet, Robert L.
  Bridging the divide : the continuing conversation between a Mormon and an Evangelical / Robert L. Millet, Gregory C.V. Johnson ;
foreword by Craig L. Blomberg and Stephen E. Robinson.
    p. cm.
  ISBN 978-0-9766843-6-7
  1. Church of Jesus Christ of Latter-day Saints--Doctrines. 2.
Mormon Church--Doctrines. 3. Evangelicalism. I. Johnson, Gregory C. V. II. Title.

BX8635.3.M548 2007
280'.042--dc22

                        2007028694

                   10 9 8 7 6 5 4 3 2 1

Bulk purchase discounts for educational or promotional purposes
are available.

            Monkfish Book Publishing Company
                   27 Lamoree Road
                Rhinebeck, New York 12572
                www.monkfishpublishing.com

To Dr. Craig L. Blomberg and Dr. Stephen E. Robinson:

For their courage in helping modern Evangelicals and
Latter-day Saints to begin a brand new conversation.

And to the Wonderful Women in our Lives:

Our Wives: Shauna and Jill
Our Mothers: Clodette and Bobbie
Our Daughters: Angie, Becky,
Indiana, California, and America

Contents

FOREWORD

I N 1992, GREG Vettel Johnson was the Student
Council President as a graduating senior at
Denver Theological Seminary. With a lifelong
interest in the Church of Jesus Christ of Latter-day
Saints and because he hoped to go into Evangelical
Christian ministry in Utah, he kept abreast of literature coming out of LDS publishing houses much
more so than probably anyone else in the Seminary
community. Stephen Robinson, Professor of Ancient Scripture at Brigham Young University, had
recently published his best-selling blockbuster, *Are
Mormons Christians?* (Salt Lake City: Deseret, 1991)
and Greg thought it deserved the attention of the
Denver faculty. In fact, he even organized a public forum on a Saturday night in which four of the
professors divided up the book with each respond-

ing to those sections that dovetailed most with his areas of expertise. Craig Blomberg was one of those four professors. The forum drew so much interest from the community that the Seminary chapel was packed.

Greg then sent the audiotape to Stephen for his response. Stephen, in turn, offered a detailed written analysis of the comments of each of the four different speakers. That led to an ongoing correspondence between Stephen and Craig, to our meeting each other face-to-face at subsequent professional conferences, to hosting each other as guests in the other's home, and eventually to opportunities for Craig to speak to the Religious Education faculty at Brigham Young University and for Stephen to address the Denver Seminary faculty. En route, the idea for the book, *How Wide the Divide? A Mormon and an Evangelical in Conversation* (InterVarsity Press, 1997) was birthed. In it, we identified four key areas of doctrinal division between most Evangelicals and most Latter-day Saints—Scripture, God and humanity, Christ and the Godhead/Trinity, and salvation. We committed to writing four chapters, one on each of these topics, in which each of us would author half of the chapter and each of us would tackle three subtopics in each of our half-chapters: what our particular community believes, often-held misconceptions about those beliefs by outsiders, and why we still remain at least partly unconvinced by the other group's position on the topic. We took turns going first so that there would be as much parity as possible. We also wrote the Introduction together. At the recommendation of the publisher, we committed to jointly authoring short conclusions to each main chapter and an overall conclusion to the whole book, which forced us to agree on the wording in which we set forth those things we discovered we had in common and those things on which we still disagreed.

The title *How Wide the Divide?* also came to us as a suggestion from InterVarsity Press. They and we intended it as a genuine question that readers should try to answer for themselves, based on the contents of the book. After five years of conversations, we probably would have answered the question as to the width of the divide between Evangelicalism and Mormonism by saying, "not as much as we once thought in many areas, more than we thought in a few areas, and about what we thought in a few other areas." Quite a few critics, however, were convinced that we had the hidden agenda of blurring all significant distinctives between our two faith communities, while a handful of readers described our work as if it had been punctuated with an exclamation point rather than a question mark: How Wide the Divide! We realized that our work, despite the kind compliments of the reviewers in both of our communities who endorsed the book on or inside its covers as a pioneering or landmark effort, would have to be picked up by others were it not to go down in history merely as an eccentric curiosity!

To our encouragement, within a couple of years a small group of LDS and Evangelical professors exhibited precisely such interest. We have met fifteen times as of this writing. Our ranks have grown, invited guests have joined us periodically, occasional public forums have been spawned as a result, and additional writing projects have been generated. But no effort has been as sustained or as encouraging as the personal friendship and public conversations between Greg Johnson, now President of Standing Together, an Evangelical Christian parachurch ministry in Utah, and Dr. Robert Millet, Professor of Ancient Scripture and former Dean of Religious Education at Brigham Young University.

The present book is an edited transcript of one of their public presentations around the country and overseas (now numbering over fifty) in the last seven or eight years. They have spoken in colleges and universities, religious and secular; Evangelical and LDS churches; theological seminaries; on television, both locally in Utah with their own weekly program over a number of weeks and nationally as interviewed on the Lee Strobel Show. In each setting they always have the identical goals. As we did in *How Wide the Divide?* they want to tell the truth to each other, and thus to their audiences, about what each believes as a representative in good standing of their respective faith communities. They want to debunk misconceptions they have discovered many people often have about their beliefs. They want to avoid sidestepping the hard questions that still keep each community from believing that the other has the fullness of the Gospel. As the format of this book illustrates, they try whenever possible to leave ample periods of time for questions from the audience and the follow-up interaction that it fosters. But theirs is no typical debate. Neither is out to try to score points or win some competition. They want to dialogue, not to debate; to have a conversation, not a confrontation. Greg and Bob are passionate about modeling convicted civility—courteous, even loving interchanges among genuinely close friends over matters of the deepest personal conviction—where Ephesians 4:15 truly is brought into play: Each man speaks the truth as best he understands it in love to the other and with those who listen and then participate.

It is not surprising that some of the greatest diplomatic successes on the stage of world politics have come after not entirely dissimilar kinds of conversations. One thinks particularly of the friendship that developed between Ronald Reagan and Mikhail Gorbachev in the mid-1980s. Peace after war, whether civil or between nations, has often required such talk. Think of the Truth and Reconciliation Commissions in South Africa, in Sierra Leone and in Peru. Far too few in our world make such hard work a priority. Rarely does it occur apart from genuine relationships, if not even deep friendships. As long as we don't have any close friends who fall into category "x" (whether x is a race or a nationality or a religion or a political party or a myriad of other things), people may say whatever they want about x-ers and treat them however they like, and it will be easy for us not to be much affected or feel the need to respond. But when some of our closest friends are members of group "x," and others mistreat or misrepresent or stereotype or caricaturize them, then we find ourselves taking the matter much more personally and responding to try to correct the situation.

If you have any doubts that you know everything there is to know about either Evangelical or Latter-day Saint religion and have even the slightest desire to learn more, this book is for you. (If you're sure you do know it all, then this book is really for you, but you're not likely to be reading it in the first place, except perhaps to tell others where it's wrong!) The book is straightforward and easy to read but never simplistic; lively and at times even humorous yet without in any way trivializing the conversation; passionate but never polemical; and immensely courteous. As Stephen and I can attest, we have had more encounters than we care to recall with people who have combatively insisted that we were not combative enough with each other, with people who have excelled in decrying in a truly mean-spirited fashion our objections to those who treat one another with mean spirits! But neither of us has run into nearly enough people in our lives who have tried as hard as Bob and Greg have to speak the truth to one another in love. May they inspire many, many more of us to go and do likewise.

Craig L. Blomberg
Distinguished Professor of New Testament
Denver Seminary
Littleton, Colorado

Stephen E. Robinson
Professor of Ancient Scripture
Brigham Young University
Provo, Utah

June 2007

R ELIGION IS A tough thing to talk about, especially when there are theological differences between the participants in the conversation. Most traditional Christian groups have
managed to bend and stretch and cut one another
enough slack so that what outsiders would perceive
to be significant differences are acknowledged but
allowed under the large umbrella of Christendom.
Thus differences in such fundamental doctrines/
practices as what it takes to be saved, the involve-
ment or non-involvement of men and women in their
own conversion process, priestly hierarchies, neces-
sity of and mode of baptism and other sacraments,
manifestations of the Spirit, pre- or post-millennial-
ism, Lordship salvation, etc.—these matters are understood to be less vital than more central and sav-

ing truths, thereby permitting variation and variety among the children living under one large roof.

In recent years interfaith dialogues have gone forward between such groups as Roman Catholics and Lutherans, Catholics and Evangelicals, Orthodox and Lutherans, and Orthodox and Pentecostals. In addition, on a much more limited but worthwhile basis, meaningful conversations have gone on between Evangelicals and Latter-day Saints (Mormons). Such topics as the nature of God, the nature of fallen humanity, the work of the Atonement, the proper place of grace and works, deification, the Trinity, the status of scripture, creeds and *sola scriptura*, the place of religious authority—these and several other concepts have been addressed among a growing number of LDS and Evangelical scholars through a fruitful exchange that has been underway since the late 1990s.

In 1997, our colleagues Craig Blomberg of Denver Seminary (Evangelical) and Stephen Robinson of Brigham Young University (LDS) broke new ground through the publication of a book entitled *How Wide the Divide? A Mormon and an Evangelical in Conversation* (InterVarsity Press). The authors addressed themselves at some length to the issues of Scripture, God, Christ, and Salvation. "This is a landmark book!" said Ronald Enroth, professor of Sociology at Westmont College. "The first of its kind—an engaging dialogue between scholars of two 'opposing' religious communities presented in a context of civility and mutual respect. It will have substantial significance," Enroth continued, "both to Mormons and to Evangelicals, and is sure to generate discussion."

And indeed it did! As we would suppose, the book elicited both praise and criticism from both sides. There were those who felt as though one or the other had conceded too much, had compromised in some way, or did not represent their own faith tradition boldly or even accurately. There were those who simply felt it inappropriate for a Christian to engage in serious dialogue with one who was, by most Evangelical standards of measure, a non-Christian; to do so was to "legitimize" the LDS claim to a place under the Christian umbrella. There were Latter-day Saints who felt, on the other hand, that the Mormons had been allowed their day in court, had finally been permitted to tell their own story in a national publication.

In was in the aftermath of *How Wide the Divide?* that the two of us (Millet and Johnson) met and began our own conversations. Long, long hours and scores of visits raised questions, sent us both searching for clarification, and resulted in a valued friendship and eventually in a working partnership. Enough inquiries, accusations, and charges of misrepresentation led Bob to write a book addressing itself, in a somewhat different way, to the Christology and Soteriology of Mormonism. The result was another unusual effort in 2005, the book *A Different Jesus? The Christ of the Latter-day Saints* (Eerdmans), with Foreword and Afterword written by Richard J. Mouw, President and professor of Philosophy at Fuller Theological Seminary. Like *How Wide the Divide?*, *A Different Jesus?* brought friend and foe out of the woodwork and revived the stir of critics, an outcome that was not all bad.

This book, *Bridging the Divide, The Continuing Conversation Between a Mormon and an Evangelical*, represents another installment in the ever-widening avenue of inquiry and discussion between two faith traditions who share basic moral values (the sanctity of life, chastity, and the preservation of traditional marriage and family) but who have doctrinal differences between them. The reader will notice that the format for this book is quite different than that of the Blomberg/Robinson volume. Here we are literally involved in a conversation about who we are, how we came to this point, what we believe, and what similarities and differences exist between us. After introducing the project, we turn to one another with questions and then finally to questions posed by Latter-day Saint and Evangelical audiences over the years.

This work is based on the fact that "convicted civility" (the term used by Rich Mouw) can and should exist between Latter-day Saints and Evangelicals, especially as we consider and weigh sacred subjects, matters vital to the salvation of the soul. To be sure, no one wants to be led astray. No one wants to be guilty of compromise. At the same time, surely no one who professes a present belief in and eternal loyalty to the Lordship of Jesus Christ—who identifies themselves as one of his disciples—would condemn or block a sincere effort to better understand and love our brothers and sisters of other faiths. Jesus taught a doctrine of inclusion, a mindset that emphasized that we "judge not," meaning that we admit at the outset that we do not know the heart of another human being, that we do not grasp fully how they feel toward God and in what manner they have dedicated their lives to spreading the good news, the glad tidings of his Beloved Son.

Greg and I have known each other quite well since 1997. There are few issues of conflict and disagreement that have gone undetected and undiscussed; we have neither hidden our heads in the sand nor acted as though there were no differences. But our engagement has been undertaken in a spirit of openness (knowing that we really can learn something from the other); sincerity (knowing that only through honesty, transparency, and trust can genuine progress be made); and love (knowing that only as we seek to see and feel toward the other something of what the Master sees and feels are we prepared to minister meaningfully to one another). True religion is a thing of the heart as well as the mind, and when we tread there we tread on holy ground, ground that must not be trampled or harrowed up unnecessarily.

Some readers may be troubled by the title of this book, *Bridging the Divide*. Let us be clear: The bridge connecting Mormonism with Evangelicalism has not been completed. There are gaps, in some cases large gaps, between our respective faith positions. We have not settled all issues, and are soberly aware that we may not do so in our lifetime. But we are in the business of engaging the issues, wrestling over doctrinal matters, acknowledging differences, and rejoicing in similarities and agreements. In other words, while the bridge is under way, it obviously has not been "fitly framed together" (Ephesians 2:21).

What we agree on absolutely is this: People matter. Their feelings matter. God is in the business of people, and so must we be if we are to be successful as his under-shepherds. Our enthusiasm for spreading the truth far and wide and convincing the nations to repent and come unto Christ must never take the form of "grace in your face" or "grace up your nose" if we are to be effective ambassadors of the Prince of Peace. In the words of our friend John Stackhouse, "God cares about people more than he cares about 'truth' in the abstract. Jesus didn't die on the cross to make a point. He died on the cross to save people whom he loves. We, too, must represent our Lord with love to God and our neighbor always foremost in our concerns."

It is our hope that what follows will prove to be both intellectually stimulating and spiritually encouraging in this work of reaching out to those who do not see things exactly as we do. Our scope has been broadened, our minds expanded, our witness strengthened, and our lives enriched in ways we never could have supposed in 1997. That the reader may partake of at least a pinch of our enthusiasm for this enterprise and sense its worth is our sincere prayer.

AN INTRODUCTION
FROM REV. GREGORY JOHNSON

T HE COVER DESIGN of this book is an interesting example of how challenging it can
be to engage in inter-religious conversation and friendship. Bob, a devout Latter-day Saint,
and I, a devout Evangelical Christian, have been
working on this book project for a number of years,
and it was always our goal to offer a next installment
to the significant Blomberg/Robinson book of 1997,
*How Wide the Divide? A Mormon and an Evangeli-
cal in Conversation* (InterVarsity Press). Originally,
we thought the title of our book, *Bridging the Divide:
The Continuing Conversation between a Mormon and
an Evangelical,* would appropriately be offered as a
question and as such conclude with a question mark,
Bridging the Divide?. It was then and remains now

an important concern for me that no one misunderstands the title of our book. Neither Bob nor I would want anyone to think that we believe that the theological divide between Evangelicalism and Mormonism has been bridged, thus the need for a question mark. Lest our critics cry foul and say that Bob and I are essentially theological compromisers who are betraying our own faith traditions, we wanted to say that we are engaged in the process of bridge building. That is to say, we are two men of two different faiths, historically hostile to each other, who are building a bridge of friendship and dialogue between us in the hopes that improved communication can lead to increased understanding of each other's faith, reduced confrontationalism, and an improved ability to share the hope that resides in us in a way that is both respectful and gentle (I Peter 3:15). Of course Bob and I could do this privately without writing a book or by presenting our national dialogue, "A Mormon and an Evangelical in Conversation," (which we have done now 50 times as of this writing) but it is our sincere desire that our model of what Dr. Richard Mouw of Fuller Seminary calls "Convicted Civility" would be replicated in individual Mormon/Evangelical relationships throughout the world.

So then, the question might be asked, "Why is there no question mark at the conclusion of our title on the cover of this book?" Well, I'm glad you asked. The suggestion was made by our publisher that our book should make a statement rather than pose a question, provoke a reaction, if you will, to the very idea that a bridge of dialogue could be built between a present day LDS scholar and an Evangelical pastor. What makes the Bob Millet and Greg Johnson dialogue unique to us is that we believe we are being genuine representatives of our own faith traditions while at the same time breaking new ground in our public civility. We are not engaged, nor are we interested in what might be termed "liberal interfaith activities" or in some circles "ecumenicism." In other words, we are not attempting to play down our theological differences just to get along and be nice with one another. It is our sincere hope that an agenda greater than our own would prevail, indeed, that God would accomplish what He desires to do through this relational bridge building effort at whatever level He desires to do it. Both Bob and I have confidence that God's agenda in all of this is far superior to whatever agenda we might have begun our friendship with, and by deferring to His plan

xxvii

we are allowing the process of dialogue to continue as He directs.

Now then, back to the cover of our book. After I yielded to the no question mark suggestion, I countered by requesting that the cover of the book should picture an uncompleted bridge showing visually what the question mark would have, had it been in our title. Actually, we had always had the idea of an uncompleted bridge on the cover anyway, so I was confident that clarity would prevail and that our readers would understand that our faith conversation was a work in progress, not a completed act. In fact, Bob and I would both be troubled by the thought or implication that our book was suggesting that the divide between Mormonism and traditional/Evangelical Christianity had been bridged. And lest anyone accuse either of us of saying so, we both affirm that there are significant theological differences between our two faiths, and they are of eternal importance, but this should not prevent us from doing the hard work of discussing truth with one another in a loving and Christ-honoring way.

Well, as you can see by the cover of our book, a very lovely and long completed bridge was chosen for our cover. Now, please do not get me wrong, I like the bridge on our cover and I think it makes our cover very attractive and eye catching. Once again, my concern remains that the completed bridge might be interpreted by some as a statement that we are saying the Mormon/Evangelical divide has been bridged and is not a conversation that is underway. My disappointment over this decision was genuine, even after the suggestion was made that the length of the bridge implied that our conversation had a long way to go still, and that our title was not actually saying, "The divide between Mormonism and Evangelical Christianity has been bridged." I must say that at this point it may have appeared to Bob and Monkfish Publishing that I was just being a little stubborn, but my concerns were legitimate to me and I wanted my Evangelical constituency to understand my heart and conviction in this area. When Bob humorously asked at this point if I would be ok with an Angel Moroni statue somewhere on the bridge I replied, "Bob, that would kill the book deal!"

I began this introduction by stating that the story of our cover design was an interesting example of how interfaith friendships can be difficult. I did not share the challenges presented in selecting our cover design to be critical of my co-author or our publisher, but simply to reveal how the process works. Yes, there are things we overlook, things we put aside, matters we leave for later when we engage in cross-religious conversations with people not of our faith. Far too often, people who love to talk about truth seem to listen poorly and are unable to give any ground in the discussion. I like the line from Ravi Zacharias who once stated, "When we throw dirt at someone, two things generally happen, we get dirty and we lose ground in the process." There are ways around some of the peripheral matters of concerns between people of differing faiths, and for me, writing this introduction as an explanation of our cover and how it illustrates an important part of the process was a fair compromise. In the end, we have an attractive cover that makes a statement that might cause a reaction of curiosity, that might lead folks to buy this book, read my introduction, and understand everything I needed to say about our cover, and everyone is still happy.

Let me conclude by saying, as one who used to primarily engage Latter-day Saint people with an "apologetics only" mentality, seeking to prove them wrong by contrasting their claims with my understanding of biblical truth, that a dialogue approach is frankly more difficult but at the same time far more rewarding. In what is increasingly being called a "Missional

Model" of ministry, the task of engaging our spiritual other with "just the facts" really is not enough. If we Evangelicals are concerned about Mormon people, if we think their beliefs or their world view are contradictory to revealed biblical truth, then I think we are obligated to engage them in patient, loving, honest, dare I say, Christian conversations about truth. We must be reminded of the Apostle Paul's words in First Corinthians that while Paul or Apollos might have planted or watered the seeds of faith in the hearts of unbelievers, "God made it grow" (3:6). Thus, in frankness, it is really not my job, nor is it within my ability to make Bob Millet embrace the truth of Jesus Christ as I see it. Rather, my role is to love Bob Millet, be his friend, to pray for him, share life with him, and honor him as my fellow human being and fellow truth seeker. I will gladly leave the transformation process or any other plan that God might have in my relationship with Bob in His capable and divine hands. In the end, I have been faithful to my truth convictions, I have integrity before God as His ambassador of Good News, and I have a wonderful friendship with a man named Bob whom I hope has seen the testimony of God's amazing grace in my life. Having said that, I hope you enjoy the book. May many wonderful missional friendships be in your future!

PART I
BACKGROUNDS

GREGORY C. V. JOHNSON (GREG): In one sense, the scriptural warrant for our dialogue is found in the writings of the Apostle Peter, who instructed the early Saints to be ready at all times to provide a reason for the hope within them, but to do so "with gentleness and respect" (1 Peter 3:15, NIV).

Our very first interfaith dialogue was done at an Episcopal Church in Park City, Utah, in the year 2001. My alma mater, Westmont College, invited us to come to their campus and make this same presentation the next year. In 2003, we broke new ground historically at Utah State University in Logan, Utah with our dialogue being cosponsored by Campus Crusade for Christ and the LDS Institute of Religion. We were anticipating a small group but probably had about 350 people in attendance, a packed auditorium. It was a very fine exchange, and the students were extremely responsive. We were all blessed by the occasion.

Let me make a quick introduction, have Bob do the same, model some of the doctrinal discussions we have had in the past (over many soup and salad lunches!), and then take questions from the audience. There is, occasionally, some confusion that's generated by our presentation. Some are confused about what the whole point of this is, why we spend the time and expend the effort. Some people come to these discussions expecting a debate, an argument, a fight. In fact, I remember when we were at Westmont, reading the student newspaper the next morning: "Students gathered in Porter Hall last night anticipating a Mormon and an Evangelical debating each other, and what they got instead was two friends talking about their faiths." Now, we were complimented by that, but there is a certain tension, I think, that some within the audience didn't get what they came looking for. They were hoping for a little sparring, maybe some sparks and some conflict, to be able to leave that place saying, "Our guy got him. Didn't our guy do better than the other guy?" You know—this kind of reaction. And so if you're anticipating a theological street fight in this book, you may well be disappointed too, because that's really not our heart. It's not what we're about. We think there is a better way, a more inspiring and informative way to undertake such an exchange.

Over the last decade, Robert Millet has become a great friend. And I have shared some wonderful times with him—in conversation, interaction, travel, and personal discussions. And during all of that we've been able to talk about any religious topic, any question, any difference of our faith background in the complete, fullest sense of the word. To some degree, this process is a bit messy because it's not really clear how things are all going to turn out, how what we're trying to demonstrate will materialize. Just as a caterpillar goes into a cocoon and comes out a butterfly, we know what goes into this dialogue, and we know just what can come out of it. The means can, however, be a little uncertain and unsettling, even messy at times.

ROBERT L. MILLET (BOB): In fact, one of the frustrations we both experienced for several months was that neither one of us could discern exactly where this was heading. In other words, at what point do we stop? Do we discontinue the conversation when Greg refuses to be a Mormon? Do we stop when I refuse to be an Evangelical? Clearly that wasn't the answer. The question became one of, "Where is this going, and when will we be there, and when will we know?" We discovered, by trial and error, that those were questions that were out of our reach. To the extent that we put those issues away, placed them on the shelf for now and didn't worry about them, opportunities for better understanding, opportunities to better articulate our deepest feelings, opportunities to share with other people increased.

To be completely honest and forthright with you, I'd say that if everything we have worked to accomplish were to end now, it will have been more than worth it because of the friendship that's developed. But there's so much more to it than that. I know worlds more about Evangelicalism now, and I know worlds more about Mormonism than I ever knew before. That's one of the unanticipated benefits— one is required to re-think, re-word, and learn to re-articulate his or her own religious beliefs. While our vocabulary is often the same, the meanings may be somewhat different. In short, we've been required to learn how to communicate with a person who feels about sacred and personal things very differently than we do.

GREG: To be candid, this is a work in progress. And indeed, to some extent, we trust that God will do His work in the process of this exchange, both tonight and in the future. We hold it out as just a humble example of the kinds of things that can happen with you and your neighbors. This is a wonderful dynamic, an exchange of friendship, a building of relationship where there is no step-by-step procedure. We can just see where the Lord will take this thing. Bob, would you share a little about yourself?

BOB: I was born and raised in Baton Rouge, Louisiana, and so most all of my friends were Roman Catholic, Southern Baptist, or Methodist. Although I was brought up in The Church of Jesus Christ of Latter-day Saints, I didn't know many Mormons, at least beyond my little congregation. We worshipped in a very small LDS branch. There was a time and a season when my family was not active in the Church, and I can remember very well starting school in Nashville, Tennessee and attending a Vacation Bible School there. As I grew up, I discovered that quite a few of my cousins were Pentecostal Holiness. Some of them have worked as Pentecostal ministers.

So this is a life I have known over the years. I have felt something deep down for persons of other faiths for a long time. I know what it's like to be in the minority, in terms of religion, and so I am a bit more sensitive to those outside the LDS faith who live in Utah. The year I started the sixth grade we moved to a small town in southern Louisiana, a tiny Cajun community made up almost completely of Roman Catholics. I remember distinctly the first day of class that my teacher, Mrs. Templet, asked the question: "Now is there anyone here who is not Catholic? If so, I need to know." My heart raced and my blood pressure rose. I looked about the class in a frightened and terribly shy way. I saw one boy across the room lift his hand slowly. "What are you?" Mrs. Templet asked. "I'm a Baptist," he responded, in a voice that was just above a whisper. I sat there, clearly realizing that there was not one human being in the room besides myself who had the slightest idea what a Mormon was, including the teacher. My temptation was to sit still and be quiet. But in a twinge of conscience I slowly lifted my hand into the air. "And what are you?" the teacher asked sternly. My faith failed and my strength went down the drain as I replied timidly, "I'm a Baptist too." So I also know something about what it feels like to be "backslidden."

In 1991, not long after I was appointed dean of Religious Education at BYU, one of the leaders of the Church said to me, "You must find ways to reach out. You must find ways to build bridges of friendship and understanding with persons of other faiths." He said a number of other things to me but that one idea weighed upon me for months. We began a series of visits to other campuses. Our first visit actually was to Notre Dame. My associate dean and I spent about four or five days there trying to understand better how Notre Dame as a church institution could hold fast to its religious heritage and at the same time reach forward toward academic excellence. After that, we made contact with such schools as Baylor, Wheaton College, and Catholic University.

In April of 1997 our religion faculty invited Professor Bruce Demerest of Denver Seminary to visit Provo and speak to us. His topic was Melchizedek, which, of course, is a matter of some interest to Latter-day Saints. Besides our own faculty, two local ministers were in attendance, one of whom was Pastor Greg Johnson, who was then shepherding a small flock in Huntsville, Utah, just east of Ogden. I happened to slip into the meeting late. During the question and answer session I referred to something that had been written by John MacArthur, Pastor/Teacher at Grace Community Church in Sun Valley, California. Greg introduced himself to me after the meeting and inquired as to my interest in MacArthur's writings. I took him into my office and showed him the section of my library on Evangelical writings, including a shelf of MacArthur's books.

GREG: It was impressive. He had books by such Evangelical writers as Ravi Zacharias, Lee Strobel, Philip Yancey, Billy Graham, Chuck Swindoll, Charles Stanley, and a whole host of others.

BOB: And so we began talking, and I said, "MacArthur's someone I'd like to meet one day." Greg responded, "Well, that could probably be arranged." To make a long story short, Greg, his associate pastor, one of my associate deans, and I traveled to California a few months later, attended services on Sunday, and met with John for lunch on Monday. The four of us had a stimulating experience with John, discussing doctrinal matters for some two hours. I explained that we had no set agenda and were not exactly sure why we had chosen to visit him, except that we had admired his writings and wanted to meet him. I think we added that we had several questions we would like to pose in order to better understand Evangelical theology. I mentioned that I oversaw the teaching of religion of more than 30,000 young people at Brigham Young University and felt it would be wise for me to be able to articulate properly and accurately the beliefs of our friends of other faiths. I hoped, as well, that they might make the effort to understand our beliefs so as not to misrepresent what we teach.

I should add, at the first, that John was absolutely stunned that two LDS religion professors would visit him, but he was even more perplexed that we had read his books and enjoyed them! I took it a step farther: I indicated to him that although there were some doctrinal chasms between us, I had quoted him in quite a few of my own books. We began our discussion of one of his more controversial books (*The Gospel According to Jesus*) and shared our own feelings, as he had stated so forcefully in his work, that true faith always manifests itself in faithfulness and that too many people who claim Christian discipleship betray their lack of conversion to the Savior by their worldliness.

Early in our conversation he said something like, "Look, anyone knows there are big differences between us. But I don't want to begin with those differences. Let's talk about Christ." We then discussed faith in Christ, justification by faith, baptism, sanctification, salvation, heaven, hell, agency and predestination, premortal existence, and a number of other fascinating topics. We compared and contrasted, we asked questions, and we answered questions. In thinking back on what was one of my most productive and worthwhile learning experiences, the one thing that characterized our discussion, and the one thing that made the biggest difference, was the mood that existed there—a mood of openness, candor, and a general lack of defensiveness. We knew what we believed, and we were all committed to our own religious tradition. No one was trying to convert the other, but rather instead we were making an effort to better understand one another. This experience says something to me about what can happen when men and women of good will come together in an attitude of openness and in a sincere effort to better understand and be understood.

I can still remember a very important moment on that trip. The night before we met with MacArthur, just after dinner, we sat in my motel room and the four of us chatted together for a few hours. Either Greg or his associate said, "And so, Bob, it really bothers you, hurts you, when you hear yourselves referred to as non-Christians." I said, "It really does." And then one of them said, "Well, how do you think it makes us feel when we read what are purported to be the words of God to Joseph Smith concerning Christianity in 1820: 'All their creeds are an abomination in my sight' or when we hear that the Latter-day Saints belong to 'the only true and living church on the face of the whole earth?'" I don't know exactly what took place at that particular moment, but something happened in my heart. The shoe had been put on the other foot, and I saw things in a whole new light. Now I didn't change my beliefs, but I changed the way I felt towards persons of other faiths.

Since that time we've had many, many occasions, Greg and I, to eat together and to talk and listen together. We've both probably gained some weight through this whole process! There was much salad, many hard questions, a great deal of soul searching. As I mentioned earlier, one of the great unanticipated blessings for me has been to face the challenge of answering questions that I really hadn't thought about before and to articulate my perceptions in a way that would enable Greg (and other friends) to track me. The rewards have been tremendous.

GREG: You all need to know that I was, essentially, raised in the LDS Church. My mother was converted to the Mormon faith when I was three years old, so, for all intents and purposes, it was the Church of my upbringing. During my mid-teens I attended a summer Bible camp and had a personal experience with Jesus Christ that changed me. This new spiritual discovery led me to leave The Church of Jesus Christ of Latter-day Saints, and so I began to attend another church in our community. In time my experience led me to become an Evangelical Christian. I attended college in Santa Barbara (Westmont), then went to Denver Seminary (for an M. Div.), and in 1992 served my first pastorate in a Baptist congregation up in Ogden, Utah.

I came to Utah as a pastor because I was passionate about sharing the grace of Jesus Christ with Mormon people, and to try to cultivate better communication between Mormons and Evangelicals. The first church I served in Utah was passionate about being sensitive to the local LDS culture by building bridges of relationship and by tearing down walls. During the first six years of pastoring in the Ogden area in two different Baptist congregations, I would say I spent a lot of time growing significant friendships with Mormon people. It was during that time that one of Bob's colleagues, Stephen Robinson, and a professor friend of mine from Denver Seminary, Craig Blomberg, co-authored and released a book titled, *How Wide the Divide? A Mormon and an Evangelical in Conversation* (InterVarsity, 1997). And it was right about that time that I was able to journey down to BYU in Provo and be there with Dr. Demerest. Bob and I met on that occasion and we had the experience in his office with all his Evangelical books. I think that what was so fascinating about the trip to California to meet John MacArthur was that it was very natural. It wasn't a contrived thing. It was just an opportunity that God laid before us. I remember feeling very impressed that Bob, after our initial conversation, said, "I'd like to come up and visit your church some time." I remember thinking that my office was some two hours from BYU. Would this guy really want to drive that far just to visit? He did and we spent a fruitful afternoon in my Huntsville office, had a meal together, and it was on that occasion that I first explained to Bob why I had chosen at 14 to leave the LDS Church. Our relationship began to take shape after that. Before too long I moved down to the Provo area, which seems now to have been divinely inspired, because it provide more contact opportunities for Bob and me. We began to talk among ourselves about doing in person the very thing that Robinson and Blomberg had done in writing in *How Wide the Divide?*

There certainly have been, as Bob said, many blessings that have resulted from this interaction: to be able to articulate your faith to someone else who is not of your faith is a good discipline because you have to check your own vocabulary, your own terminology, and make sure that people can not only hear the words you're saying but can really understand. This is particularly the situation as we, with our Mormon friends, discover at times that we have a vocabulary that is very similar but find that we have different definitions and meanings for those words. So it's not an easy thing. You really have to wrestle through that process. To some degree, we have been forced to really think through our own paradigms, our own theology, our own understanding of things and know what we believe in a way that enables us to share with each other in an informative manner.

Bob: Along the way, one of the challenges we faced was inevitable: the matter of trust. That is to say, Greg might ask me a question, I would give an answer, only to notice an uncomfortable look on his face, a look that bespoke his doubt as to whether I was really stating accurately what Latter-day Saints believe. It was as if he were asking—and I've been asked this a hundred times or more by others—"Are you just saying those words, or do you really mean that?" Or if I would ask him a question, I might wonder whether most Evangelicals feel the same way or whether his response was idiosyncratic to Greg Johnson. So during the early stages, had we not been patient and persistent, we might have concluded that the other person was being disingenuous in order to keep a friendship intact.

To illustrate, we have had long conversations on grace and works. There were times when I sensed that Greg was almost believing what I said, but not quite. That is, I wasn't certain that he felt I was representing mainstream Mormonism. So in order to try to convince him, I did something rather unusual. I contacted the local BYU Continuing Education office and said to a friend of mine there that oversees lecture series beyond the BYU campus: "Frank, I need a favor." He said, "What's that?" "I need you to set up a speaking assignment in Ogden in which I give three lectures in a row." I explained that I needed to do it in and around a certain time period. "Can you do that?" I inquired. He said, "Sure." So he set it up and we picked the titles and then I called Greg on the phone. I said, "Greg, I'm going to be speaking in Ogden in a few weeks. We ought to get together, have a bite to eat, and perhaps you could join me at the lectures." He agreed and we settled on the date. Greg, why don't you describe what happened.

GREG: To be honest, I'm still not sure his speaking assignment was set up just for me. I remember that there were about 250 Latter-day Saints in attendance, and I listened as Bob gave three messages that evening, one about the Fall, one about New Birth, and the final one about Being Saved by Grace. Several times that night, I remember thinking that Bob could easily teach these messages in a Christian church minus the Book of Mormon references. Honestly, I was amazed that a lot of Mormons listening that night didn't raise some objections to the things Bob spoke about as they were not the kind of things I had heard in my LDS upbringing.

BOB: The difference was there were two hundred and fifty Latter-day Saints there, so I was making a point for Greg. What was my point?

GREG: Well, when our interfaith dialogue entails one-on-one conversation you may have a tendency to wonder about the full truthfulness of what's said.

There is, however, a certain accountability created when a BYU professor of religion speaks in front of two hundred and fifty of his own people; I would have thought that if he's saying something that's off base, somebody in the audience surely would call him on it or call someone higher in authority about it.

Bob: I think that was an important night for us because it helped to settle the fact that what I say is what I mean. What I say in private is what I would say in public. So I think one of the ways we began to grow into a meaningful friendship with each other was in the matter of trust. I came to trust that he had no ulterior motive. He came to trust that I had no ulterior motive. We believed each other. We had confidence in each other.

Greg: I think we as Evangelicals have an important thing to learn here—at some point in a relationship where trust has been gained and earned, we need to allow a person to speak for themselves and believe that they are being honest about what they are saying. Bob Millet knows, better than any other person on earth, what Bob Millet really believes. If Bob wants to tell me that he believes such and such about salvation or grace, I'm more prepared than I was ten years ago to accept that as his own personal confession and to do so with the knowledge that he's being honest with me. That's been a great discovery.

BOB: Greg often asks an important question, one that is very fair: "I believe that you believe that, Bob, but would you say it is typically believed by most Latter-day Saints?" With tongue in cheek, I sometimes say: "Well, if they don't, they should." The way I tried to demonstrate that to Greg in the lecture series in Ogden was to turn primarily to the Book of Mormon for doctrinal support of the points I was making. Teaching principally from a "foundational LDS text" rather than using Galatians or Romans (which I could have done just as easily) served to buttress my point that I was being true and loyal to LDS doctrine. It's not uncommon to have someone respond to one of my answers like this: "But that's not what your missionaries told us." I'm not quite sure yet what the best response to that comment is. For one thing, these young men and women are just that—they're young. They are remarkably devoted youth who have a strong conviction of what they are doing. I've been there. I know what they feel. It's important to realize, in addition, that their reading material and their research skills are narrow and rather limited. They are not trained theologians, nor does the Church in any way claim they are. They are humble servants called to bear testimony of certain fundamental propositions. It is not expected that they will have the answers to all of your questions or mine.

GREG: I think it's fair to say that the tension that exists whenever an Evangelical and a Latter-day Saint sit down to talk is based upon the historical relationship (or lack of relationship) that Mormons and Evangelicals have had for a long time; we have some very strong feelings about each other's beliefs: about whether or not Latter-day Saint doctrine is justifiably Christian or whether or not an Evangelical perspective is a legitimate Christian form. Stephen Robinson was invited to Denver Seminary in 1992 to discuss his book *Are Mormons Christians?* (Bookcraft, 1991) in a forum held by the seminary. Stephen was more than a little uncomfortable to do so. He learned that four Evangelical professors and he would be involved in the conversation and chose not to accept the invitation. He was very concerned about negative attitudes he would encounter.

When I was able to speak to Stephen, I said, "Well, Dr. Robinson, obviously I don't embrace Joseph Smith as an inspired latter-day prophet and don't believe it is important to embrace the Book of Mormon as scripture. Yet I believe I'm a Christian. I've had a born again experience. I love Jesus Christ. I'm preparing in seminary for a full time ministry. Am I a Christian, Dr. Robinson? Am I a Christian from your perspective?" He kind of hemmed and hawed a little bit and he said, "Well, it's like this. You're like a 60-watt light bulb and I'm a 100-watt light bulb." And I said, "Ok, let me be honest with you: if I'm a 60-watt light bulb and you're a 100-watt light bulb and I could be a 100 watt light bulb, I'd like to be. But the mere fact that you don't think I am, defines the reality that you think there's a significant difference between us. And I'm okay with that, the same way that many Evangelicals do not believe Mormonism to be Christian. You surely must realize that being called a 60-watt bulb is not very flattering, either."

Bob: And you ought to know that I've never said such a thing to Greg. I've told him that he's at least a 70-watt light bulb.

Greg: Debates between Mormons and Evangelicals have been a common thing, and you can certainly draw a crowd when you have that kind of an event because people want to see the fists fly. But to engage at this relational level is much more difficult to achieve. But I assure you that it's much more productive. One of the challenges, and I speak to the Evangelical community here, is we need to value the process in our evangelistic effort. Not every relationship we have with someone outside of our faith is going to end up with their conversion to Christianity and that needs to be understood. Too many believe that if this relationship doesn't end in a conversion or if I don't sense this person is going to convert then the relationship cannot have a long term purpose. I think we need to engage in one another's lives, really with the value of saying that this is a fellow human being. I can learn from him, and he can learn from me. And as we seek to try to communicate our own faith and our own values, we can trust that ultimately God's in charge of moving things in whatever direction or at whatever pace He chooses to move them. It was the Apostle Paul who said, "I have planted, Apollos watered; but God gave the increase" (1 Corinthians 3:6). Let me illustrate. One of Bob's colleagues became intrigued with our relationship and invited me to lunch just off the BYU campus. We sat down and had a little spaghetti, and the professor said: "Tell me what's going on with

you and Bob Millet." I shared a little bit more about
our friendship and some of the interactions we were
having. And he said, "Well, let me get to the point,
Greg. I think you are aware that Robert Millet is
the dean of our religion faculty." I said, "Of course."
"Surely you don't think he's going to convert to the
Evangelical Christian way of life, do you?" I said,
"You know, to be honest with you, I'm pretty sure
he's not." He said, "Well, I'm assuming that as an
Evangelical pastor you're not considering becoming
LDS." I said, "No, I'm not." In a moment of frustration he blurted out, "Well, what's the point?" I think
this was a God thing, a kind of inspired moment,
because I looked right at him and said, "You know
what? You're the point. If people like you continue
to have that kind of attitude about relationships like
Bob and I have, then we'll never have the opportunity to really explore what we believe and understand
and learn together. We must see the value of such
relationships beyond conversion, that somehow
there's something meaningful about understanding
someone who believes differently than I do, that we
can put aside our agenda and let God bring to pass
His own purposes. We have decided to let God be
God, let God set the agenda, let God determine the
outcome. Such an approach brings enormous free-

dom in the way that we've been able to grow our relationship because. . ."

Bob: There's no pressure, no goals to achieve, no
conquest to make.

GREG: Sure, and because I have chosen to trust
the Lord with Bob's spiritual condition and from his
perspective, he is doing the same.

Bob: I feel no pressure to move this in a certain
direction. Greg doesn't either. Now, to be honest, in
our heart of hearts, nothing would make Bob Millet happier than witnessing Greg Johnson's baptism
into my Church, and nothing would please Greg
more than seeing me come to his way of thinking
completely.

GREG: At Utah State University there was a humorous moment because a headline in the school
newspaper was supposed to read "Come and hear
A Mormon and an Evangelical in Conversation."
Instead it read, "Come and hear a Mormon and an
Evangelical in Conversion." We each tried to persuade the audience that it was the other one that
was planning on doing the converting.

BOB: A few years ago, Greg and I traveled together to Boston. I'd been invited back to speak at an educational conference in that area and I also wanted to meet Dr. Haddon Robinson at Gordon-Conwell Seminary. Greg had known him at Denver Seminary, where Haddon had served as President of the Seminary. So Greg made arrangements for us to meet with him on Friday. The first night we arrived in Boston, a Thursday night, we set off from the airport in search of either our hotel or the Cambridge LDS Institute of Religion, where I was expected to be speak at 7:00 p.m. Now the Lord will one day need to forgive me for the feelings I had that evening toward the city of Boston. The roads were ripped up, construction was underway everywhere, and. . .

GREG: We got lost.

BOB: We got lost over and over and over again. I had so many people say, "You can't miss it." I finally stopped someone and said, "Please don't tell me that. I assure you, we can miss it." At about 7:15 or 7:20 we're still circling, looking for the Institute of Religion. During the middle of all this, Greg and I continued a conversation we have had many times on how our respective faith traditions view things, in this case how sacred things are known. It's not uncommon for me to be told by someone who is Evangelical, "Well, you know how you Mormons are: you say to someone, 'Here, look at this page in the Book of Mormon, get on your knees, pray about it, and see if you get a warm feeling.'" In other words, what I've been told over and over is that Mormonism depends upon conversion that comes solely through an emotional experience. I thought for a minute, turned to Greg, and said: "Do you believe in the literal bodily resurrection of Jesus?" And of course the look on his face was one of "Duh." He said, "Yes, of course I do." I said, "Well, that's good, Greg. Why do you believe in the literal bodily resurrection of Jesus?" "Because the Bible teaches that Jesus rose from the dead. The New Testament witnesses of its truthfulness." "Oh, okay. Why should you trust the Bible? How do you know the Bible's true?" And then the conversation got really interesting. Greg said something like, "I know because there are so many tangible, verifiable evidences for the truthfulness of the Bible, in terms of history and culture and anthropology and archaeology and so on." It was quite an impressive list of reasons why. And then I said, " Let me tell you a story.

"I have a friend, an older woman who lives in Montgomery, Alabama. She's Evangelical Christian, and my heart goes out to her." He said, "Why's that?" I said, "I just feel sad for her." "Why do you feel sad for her?" "This is a lady that's devoted her life to Christ," I noted. "She gave her soul to the Savior 55 years ago. She's been as faithful a Christian as you'd ever want to see. She's a tremendous contributor to her congregation. She's an instrument of the Lord's peace. She's just a good person. But I just feel sad for her." He said, "Again, why do you feel sad for her?" I said, "Well, because she loves the Bible and yet can never know that the Bible's true." Greg asked, "Why can't she know that?" Greg pursued. I said, "Well, she doesn't know anything about these evidences. She probably can't say the word anthropology. I don't think she knows anything about the languages, culture, or history underlying the New Testament story. So, bless her heart, she can never have faith in Christ, can never know of the truthfulness of the bodily resurrection because she can't know the Bible's true."

Greg then said, "Well of course she can. She can know the Bible's true." I said, "No, no. Clearly the only way she can know the Bible's true is if she was aware of the kind of evidences you mentioned." He said, "No, no, don't misunderstand me, Bob. Your friend can still trust the Bible is God's Word because of her faith and because of the reality of its truthfulness whether her intellect knows all the facts or not. The facts that prove the Bible to be truthful are a confirmation to her faith. People can have faith in things that are true and faith in things that are not true." I said, "Now by that you don't mean to tell me she could have the Spirit of God witness to her soul that the Bible is true." And he said, "Sure, I would say that, but her faith is in something that can be reasonably asserted." I said, "Then we've come full circle." And this opened up a conversation between us that I think was one of the most productive conversations we've ever had. When I talk to a person and say, "Read the Book of Mormon, ponder it, pray over it, and try to gain a witness by the power of the Holy Spirit that it's true," we're talking about the same thing. We then discussed the fact that this exchange really does typify a problem. How we tend to. . .

GREG: Define our differences by extreme.

BOB: That's right: we tend to react and then stereotype another person or religious group. Greg and I concluded that Evangelicals are prone, in recent years in particular, to get really hyped up about rational evidence, to such extent that the feeling or pietistic dimension to faith is unnecessarily diminished. I admitted that there are cases where Latter-day Saints seem to be hyped up on emotion and thus do not pay enough attention to tangible, physical evidence that must underlie the witness. That is, I have no right to say that I have true faith, saving faith in Christ, if in fact there was no physical resurrection. There must be a moment in time, in the days of Pontius Pilate, in a place called Jerusalem, where the actual person of Jesus of Nazareth suffered and bled and died and atoned for the sins of the world and then, three days later, rose triumphantly from the tomb with a physical, resurrected body. I turned to Greg and said: "Of course it matters that it actually happened, but I refuse to allow my spiritual witness of the truthfulness of that singular event to be held hostage by what science has or has not discovered at the present moment."

GREG: What I think Bob's really trying to point out is that classically, as we have interacted with each other, Evangelicals have often described Mormon epistemology as a totally subjective experience—a prayer, a feeling, and then a commitment. We Evangelicals tend to be rationally driven, prone to produce a certain list of theological statements and then indicate that if your theology doesn't line up with these twelve statements, there's no way your perspective could be true or trustworthy. And we end up missing each other, like ships passing in the night. Yet we need to acknowledge that each of our traditions should be built upon evidence, both physical and spiritual. Latter-day Saints need to think about their faith, interact with their faith, study their text, ask good questions. And Evangelicals likewise need to see that we have a simple faith based, not only upon physical evidence, but also our Spirit-driven trust in the Bible. This particular topic has created much tension between Latter-day Saints and Evangelicals, when in fact our epistemologies need not be worlds apart.

In one of his recent books, *Grace Works* (Deseret Book, 2003), Bob tells the story of preparing to leave on a full-time mission. Before leaving his home in Louisiana, he asked his father, "Dad, what does it mean to be saved by grace?" His father said, "We don't believe in that." Bob asked: "Why don't we believe in it?" And his dad quickly responded, "Because the Baptists do!" And you know, I wonder to what extent we Evangelicals and Mormons have been doing the same thing to each other for a long time. We react to each other's theological emphases or how we're living out our faith, and we almost conclude that if, doctrinally speaking, the Mormons are headed east then we had better head west. And vice versa. And so if the Mormons are going to stress the need to feel a burning in the bosom after prayer, we will stress the need to pile up the physical evidences.

And that's where we can, I think, through the experience of relationship-building, go the extra mile in attempting to better understand where the other is coming from. I can say, "You know what, Bob, I appreciate the approach that you're taking and I can certainly understand that you're not going to let your faith be held captive just by scientific evidences, because as a Christian I wouldn't either. 'For without faith,' the scripture says, 'It is impossible to please God. And those that come to him must believe that he is and that he is the rewarder of those who diligently seek him' (Hebrews 11:6)." Bob has engaged in some deep thinking with me, and we've both been blessed by this learning experience.

BOB: Dr. Randall Balmer, an Evangelical historian at Barnard College of Columbia, in his little book *Growing Pains* (Brazos, 2001), gives an illustration that is very instructive. A young man happens into his professor's office and says, "Professor X, I'm not sure that I believe in God." And so what does he, as the believing but intellectually-trained professor, do? He asks the student to be seated and proceeds to give him the cosmological, ontological, and teleological proofs for the existence of God. Frankly, all the boy needed is to have someone older, wiser, and more experienced put his arm around him and say, "You know, I understand what you're feeling right now, because I remember a time when I went through that myself. In fact let me tell you how I came to faith."

Well, enough on that. We were disagreeing on a matter on which disagreement was unnecessary. To be sure—and we don't want to be suggesting otherwise—there are major differences between our two faith traditions, but let's disagree on the right things, on the real differences between us, not on supposed or trumped-up or reactionary differences. And let's do so in a civil and respectful manner.

GREG: Let us assure you that our road to real relationship has not come without several bumps along the way. Bob invited me to do an extraordinary thing—to speak in a Friday faculty forum and share my story of why I left the LDS faith with the faculty of Religion at BYU. I was amazed. He wanted me to share my testimony in front of 60 or 70 LDS faculty. He was very encouraging. Bob thought this would be a worthwhile exercise for the faculty to have.

Five days before that event took place it was cancelled because there was someone on the faculty who was very uncomfortable with such a thing. In an effort to respond appropriately to that discomfort, and to try to keep peace on the faculty, the forum was cancelled. I was deeply disappointed. Bob was heartsick.

And yet you know what was the great thing about that was that I found Bob to be my greatest encouragement: he called and said, " I really want to apologize to you because I think this would have been an extremely valuable experience for our faculty. And maybe we're not ready for it yet, but let's keep working towards it." Therefore when we test the limits there are misunderstandings, and people who will just say—and we as Evangelicals will do this often—"What's the point of this if it's not to prove the other guy wrong? What's the point of this if it's not to convert the person to our faith and way of life? What's the point of it?" Well, again, I think we have an amazing God at work, and we can let Him be in charge of making the point.

PART II
QUESTIONS FOR ONE ANOTHER

BOB: We'd like to give you a feel for how we have spent the last several years, namely, asking and answering questions. In the process, we have learned some great information but also, as we suggested earlier, we have come to appreciate the dialogue itself, inasmuch as it has helped to forge our friendship. Greg, why don't you start us off with a doctrinal question.

GREG: Okay. Bob, I know it's painful for your folks to hear us say that you are not Christian, that you do not fit within the historical framework of Christian churches. Isn't it true, however, that Latter-day Saints are basically saying the same thing about Evangelicals, and all other Christian churches for that matter, when you speak of yourselves as the "only true church" or when Jesus is supposed to have said to Joseph Smith that "all their creeds are an abomination in my sight"?

BOB: Well, I'm glad we started things off with an easy one! In the first section of the Doctrine and Covenants, a revelation given to Joseph Smith in November 1831, The Church of Jesus Christ of Latter-day Saints is in fact referred to as "the only true and living church upon the face of the whole earth" (D&C 1:30). Admittedly, this is strong language; it is hard doctrine, words that are offensive to persons of other faiths. Let me deal first with what I think the phrase does not mean. It does not mean that men and women of other Christian faiths are not sincere believers in truth and genuine followers of the Christ. Latter-day Saints have no difficulty whatsoever accepting one's personal affirmation that they are Christian, that they acknowledge Jesus Christ as the divine Son of God, their Savior, the Lord and Master of their life. Nor are Latter-day Saints the only ones entitled to personal illumination and divine guidance for their lives. It does not mean we believe that most of the doctrines in Catholic or Protestant Christianity are false or that the leaders of the various branches of Christianity have improper motives.

It does not mean that the Bible has been so corrupted that it cannot be relied upon to teach us sound doctrine and provide an example of how to live. Now, while Latter-day Saints do not believe that one can derive divine authority to perform the saving ordinances (sacraments) from the scriptures, we do say that the Bible contains the fullness of the gospel in the sense that (1) it teaches of groups of people in the past who enjoyed the full blessings of the everlasting gospel; and (2) it teaches (especially the New Testament) the good news or glad tidings of redemption in Christ through the Atonement (3 Nephi 27:13-21; D&C 76:40-42).

It does not mean that God disapproves of or rejects all that devoted Christians are teaching or doing, where their heart is, and what they hope to accomplish in the religious world. It does not mean that God-fearing Christians who are not Latter-day Saints will not go to heaven. Mormons do not in any way minimize or deny the reality of another person's experience with the Spirit of God, nor do we question the legitimacy of another's commitment to Jesus Christ. It does not mean that Latter-day Saints desire to "do their own thing" or face social challenges on their own. To be sure, we strive earnestly to work together with men and women of other faiths to stand up and speak out against the rising tide of immorality and ethical relativism that are spreading in our world.

Well then, what does "only true church" mean? More than anything else, it means that divine institutional authority (that we call priesthood) has been restored through Joseph Smith and that such power rests with the leadership of our Church. It means that doctrinal finality rests with apostles and prophets, not theologians or scholars. One professor of religion at a Christian institution once remarked to me: "You know, Bob, one of the things I love about my way of life as a religious academician is that no one is looking over my shoulder to check my doctrine and analyze the truthfulness of my teachings. Because there is no organizational hierarchy to which I am required to answer, I am free to write and declare whatever I choose." I nodded kindly and chose not to respond at the time. I have thought since then, however, that what my friend perceives to be a marvelous academic freedom can become license to interpret, intuit, or exegete a scriptural passage in a myriad of ways, resulting in interpretations as diverse as the backgrounds, training, and proclivities of the persons involved. There are simply too many ambiguous sections of scripture to "let the Bible speak for itself." In many cases, neither linguistic training nor historical background will automatically produce the (divinely) intended meaning or clarification of biblical passages. Who decides which interpretation is that which Matthew or Paul or Jesus himself intended? Further, who decides who decides? What is the standard by which we judge and interpret? Latter-day Saints believe the final word on prophetic interpretation rests with prophets.

According to one of the accounts of Joseph Smith's First Vision (1838), Joseph learned that "all their creeds were an abomination in his sight." This statement is, of course, considered to be harsh and hurtful to members of other Christian churches. Let's see if we can clarify things somewhat. For example, what were the "creeds" spoken of? Originally the Latin word credo meant simply "I believe." In Joseph Smith's day, the word creed referred to a brief summary of the articles of Christian faith or that which is believed. Clearly there is nothing wrong with a creed per se. Joseph Smith was not necessarily opposed to religious creeds in general. Latter-day Saints believe that the creeds spoken of in the First Vision were the post-New Testament creeds that sought to codify beliefs concerning God, Christ, the Holy Spirit, and their relationships, concepts that had evolved during the time following the deaths of the original apostles.

To the extent that creeds perpetuate falsehood, particularly concerning the nature of the Godhead, then of course our Father in heaven would be displeased with them. To the extent that creeds divide people, categorize people, exclude people, and even lead others to persecute them, one can appreciate why they would be viewed as undesirable. To the extent that they become a badge of belonging, the identifying mark by which a "true Christian" is known, the only way by which one can understand what the scriptures really mean about God and Christ—then to that extent the Christian circle is drawn smaller and smaller and that grace of God that makes salvation available to all humankind (Titus 2:11) is frustrated. In other words, it seems to me that God and the Prophet Joseph were about as concerned with creedalism as they were with incorrect doctrine within the creeds.

BOB: Let me ask you one, Greg. What exactly is an Evangelical? I was brought up in the deep South, and all I ever heard of traditional Christianity is that it was made up of either Catholics or Protestants.

GREG: First of all, let's get a historical perspective. In the first century, followers of Jesus began to associate and identify themselves as a group. The Acts of the Apostles tells us that they became known as "the Way," probably in reference to Jesus' statement in John 14:6 about Him being the Way, the Truth, and the Life. In time, the Way became known simply as the Christian Way or Christianity, and this was the case for over a thousand years.

Presently, there are three major historic branches of Christianity that have emerged since the days of Jesus: The Roman Catholic Church, the Orthodox Churches, and the Protestant Churches which broke from the Catholic Church in the 1500s. Evangelicals are a sub-category of the Protestant branch of Christendom, although they cannot simply be defined as Protestants or of one particular denomination. Rather, the term Evangelical has emerged over the last fifty or so years to identify an element from within the Protestant Church and from a variety of denominations. Evangelicals are known to be fundamentally committed to the authority of the Bible as God's Word and that Christian salvation comes by faith alone in Christ alone.

Evangelicals are also known to be committed to an enthusiastic proclamation of the Good News of

Jesus Christ. Evangelicals would differ from Liberal Protestants on the one hand and from Fundamentalist Protestants on the other. We would feel Liberal Protestants have forsaken clear teachings and Biblical truths that are fundamental to true Christianity. On the other hand, Evangelicals would be concerned that those identified as Fundamentalist are too exclusive in their doctrinal creed and fail to embrace humanitarian efforts, for example, that support our witness of Christ. Of course, my definition is simplistic, but it gets to the differences that exist between Evangelicals, Liberals, and Fundamentalists. So then, Evangelicals are transdenominational—they can be Baptist, Presbyterians, Assemblies of God, Evangelical Free, Methodist, Lutherans, and most any other Protestant denomination. Rather than being defined by denomination, we Evangelicals seek to be known as a people committed to Biblical Truth, who strive to share the truth with others in word and in deed. Many Latter-day Saints are quite surprised to learn that there are approximately 700 million Evangelicals around the world.

GREG: Bob and I have talked often about the nature of the Fall, in an effort to understand what happened in the Garden of Eden. Let me ask you this, Bob: What is the condition of men and women before God? What is the nature of human beings? Mormonism has a teaching that has troubled us Evangelicals, the idea that the Fall was a good thing. As I recall, one of your early leaders called the Fall a "fall upward." The idea that the Fall is a "fall up-ward" is troubling to biblical Christianity. The Bible says that the Fall was a horrible event, a moment of separation and death between God and human-kind with horrible consequences. Bob, how could the Fall ever be considered good? The Bible teaches us that all human beings are sinners and that none of us does good. What is the LDS perception of the nature of human beings?

Bob: If you were just to walk up to me and ask, What is the nature of man? you might notice an un-comfortable pause. That's a tough question for Lat-ter-day Saints. I would have to say to you, "Okay, which man do you mean?" Joseph Smith certainly taught that we are sons and daughters of God, spirit children of a Heavenly Father and that from God we inherit certain capacities, attributes, and abilities, al-beit in a rudimentary and embryonic stage. We have the capacity to acquire those attributes, to become "partakers of the divine nature" over time through the powers of Christ's Atonement. In that sense we might say that man's spirit is good by nature, for he is related to and a product of the Greatest Good, God himself. But, unfortunately the scriptures don't speak about the eternal nature a great deal; most of the time the scriptures, both ancient and modern for us, deal with what we call mortal and fallen man.

I would have to admit that the LDS perspective on the Fall is remarkably optimistic in the Christian world. Let me correct slightly your characterization of our doctrine: I'm not aware of anyone saying that Adam and Eve's act produced a fall upward, but what was said was this: the Fall had a twofold direction—downward yet forward. We believe that the Fall was a part of God's eternal plan, what Milton called a "fortunate fall." In his book, *Miracles*, C.S. Lewis postulated if we could find among the myriads of planets out there an unfallen world, that through the ministry of Jesus redeemed humanity will always rise higher than unfallen humanity and come to "bless Adam's fall." Now we don't establish our theology by what C.S. Lewis said, but we do believe that the Fall is inextricably linked to the Atonement, and that Jesus' substitutionary offering doesn't just balance the scales of justice and mercy; the Atonement serves a rehabilitative and a building function in our lives, molding and empowering us into people of purity and purpose. In the words of the Church leader you misquoted slightly, the Fall "brought man into the world and set his feet on progression's highway." A Book of Mormon prophet said it this way: "Adam fell that men might be, and men are that they might have joy."

Latter-day Saints do not believe in an "original sin." We do not believe it to be a scriptural doctrine but rather one formulated largely by St. Augustine. But there was a Fall, it does take a toll, and you will find in our literature reference to what is called being "conceived in sin." For one thing, man is conceived into a world of sin. In addition, conception becomes the vehicle or the means by which a fallen nature, mortality, what the scripture calls "the flesh" is transmitted to the posterity of Adam and Eve. I recognize that this is a pretty fine distinction— while the word depraved does make us nervous, we are much more comfortable with the concept of "human inability"—the fact that men and women cannot, simply cannot, forgive or cleanse or redeem or renew or save themselves. That is the work of God. We do believe we can cooperate with the Almighty in that endeavor through the exercise of faith in Christ, but we are painfully aware of our spiritual inabilities and limitations. There was a fall, and it takes its toll spiritually, physically, emotionally, intellectually, and every other way. Our only hope for deliverance from death and hell and sin is through the redemption offered by Christ. The Fall and the Atonement are companion doctrines, a package deal. And so ours is a fairly positive view of the Fall—we see it as necessary, something that opened the door for mortality, but something that needs to be overcome, something that creates a nature that must be changed from the inside out. Ezra Taft Benson taught that just as a man does not really desire food until he is hungry, so he does not desire the salvation of Christ until he know why he needs Christ. And no one know why he needs Christ unless and until he understands the doctrine of the Fall and its effect upon all mankind.

GREG: When you look at Romans 5 and understand that whole first Adam and second Adam teaching, then the doctrine of the Fall is, for Evangelicals, so vital because it helps us realize just how broken we are, how bent our souls are. Then and only then can we truly understand the magnificence of what Jesus has done for us. Jesus didn't just help us out of a little unfortunate situation; He has resuscitated us. Jesus didn't come just to make bad men good men, but He came to make dead men live again. This insight enables us to grasp the powerful significance of salvation.

As Evangelicals we have different traditions. Certainly there's a Reformed position where persons believe we are elected to faith in Christ through God's divine sovereignty. Some would say that our sinful condition is so bent that we don't even have the ability to choose God; we therefore need a kind of prevenient grace, a special divine assistance to empower us toward an acceptance of Christ's salvation. Other Evangelicals feel that we each have free will and thus the capacity to choose for ourselves, to choose Jesus Christ as our Lord and Savior. I acknowledge that those are pretty big differences between Evangelicals. I think both Arminian and Reformed folks would, however, affirm the fall of man as a horrific thing that happened in the Garden of Eden, an event resulting in a major separation between God and man. As Paul said in Ephesians 2, while we were dead in our trespasses we are made alive in Christ Jesus. That's something that's fundamental in Evangelical theology.

Bob: I think I would just say this. There is a temptation on the part of some Latter-day Saints to not take the Fall seriously enough. If you do not take it seriously, you may be prone to see Jesus as a kind of celestial cheerleader, a spiritual adviser or consultant, rather than as a Savior and Redeemer, one who comes on a search and rescue mission for us, our only hope for deliverance and salvation. So I think you and I probably disagree as to the intent of the Fall. On the other hand, we are not far off doctrinally when it comes to discussing the effects of the Fall and the need for divine assistance.

Bob: Greg, let me ask you a different but related question. One of the issues raised most often by my students is this: There appears to be in the Evangelical world a tremendous emphasis upon—what shall we call it?—the altar call, the formal movement to the front to accept Jesus, the confession of Christ with the lips, but not a great deal of emphasis upon discipleship after that acceptance. Latter-day Saints sometimes wonder, once you've accepted Christ, if Evangelicals feel it doesn't matter how you live thereafter, for your salvation is secure. Would you like to respond to that?

GREG: Of course I've heard that as well. Many times a Latter-day Saint or anyone else, for that matter, may wonder whether we Evangelicals almost have a "trust Jesus, live like hell, and then go to heaven" approach to life. In other words, once you've accepted Jesus you can just live any way you want. I think that's a real problem and a major misunderstanding, because certainly clear biblical teaching is that true justification, when that takes place in a person's life, results in genuine transformation, little by little, precept by precept. It's unfortunate that occasionally within Evangelical circles there should exist a type of easy believism that can result from our lack of emphasis on the reality and the importance of discipleship and the calling of the new believer to count the cost.

BOB: A kind of "cheap grace?" Recently I read two different books by Evangelicals that expressed concern that one of the reasons born again Christians do not seem to be living any differently on the whole than non-Christians is that the concept of grace has been grossly misunderstood. In an effort to insure that absolutely nothing be added to the "finished work" of Christ, some have overlooked the fundamental fact that coming unto Christ entails obedience, requires discipleship. One book was by Ron Sider and called *The Scandal of the Evangelical Conscience* (Baker, 2005), and the other was by Robert Jeffress, called, interestingly, *Grace Gone Wild* (Waterbrook Press, 2005).

GREG: Yes, a cheap grace. I know that was an important issue for you when you read John Mac Arthur's book, *The Gospel According to Jesus*. That book certainly generated a great deal of interest and hot conversation. I would say, clearly, that it is our deepest commitment as Evangelicals to believe that we're saved by grace alone through faith, as stated in Ephesians 2:8-9. From our perspective, when it comes to a person's salvation, 100% of the credit belongs to Jesus. And yet, Bob, when a person's life is truly transformed by a full acceptance of the good news of Jesus Christ, as James says, that inner change will be evidenced by good works. I think it's an unfortunate misconception that Evangelicals will sometimes communicate in their attempt to solidify the notion of salvation by grace alone. Once saved by faith, then the good works flow from a regenerated heart, as Ephesians 2:10 states.

BOB: What would you conclude, then, if a person was saved on 12 January 2002 and continued to live what could be called an extremely sinful life? Would you conclude that true conversion had never really taken place?

GREG: That would certainly be the temptation. If that person claims to have accepted Jesus with their whole heart but there are clear violations of that commitment, repeated offenses against the ten commandments, for example, such that their lifestyle does not seem to be in harmony with their profession, I would be prone to suggest that that person may not have made a sincere commitment to Christ in the first place. At some point it might be appropriate to challenge them to exercise some level of church discipline and say: "You cannot continue to call yourself a Christian if you have no intention of letting Jesus change your heart and have his way in your life."

GREG: I think obviously I can flip this issue right back to you and say that our concern as Evangelicals is that Latter-day Saints seem to have placed too great an emphasis on being righteous and working out their own salvation. Mormons are fond of quoting from the Book of Mormon that "We're saved by grace, after all we can do." Do you believe that you're saved by grace or by works?

BOB: If you were to ask me, "Do you believe we are saved by grace alone?" I would have responded with an unequivocal Yes and No. Salvation, according to both the Book of Mormon and the Doctrine and Covenants, along with the Bible, is the greatest of all the gifts of God. You don't earn a gift.

GREG: I couldn't agree more, but talk to me some more about this.

BOB: From a Latter-day Saint perspective, the gospel of Jesus Christ is a gospel covenant, a two-way promise between God and man. On one side, God promises to do for us those things we could never do for ourselves: forgive our sins, cleanse our heart, renew our nature, raise us from the grave in the resurrection, and glorify us for heaven hereafter. These are matters over which I have absolutely no control, matters of pure grace. For us grace is not just that final boost into the celestial kingdom that comes at the end of one's life but also an enabling power that assists us to do things every day of our lives, all along the way, that we could not do on our own. The passage in 2nd Nephi that we've become famous for—that we're saved by grace, after all we can do—has, I fear, been misunderstood by many Latter-day Saints and especially by many not of our faith. Too many Latter-day Saints read or quote that passage and suppose God cannot help them until they've done everything they can do. Then He will kick in, or fill in the gaps. I am persuaded from the larger doctrinal context of the Book of Mormon that the phrase "after all we can do" means above and beyond all we can do, notwithstanding all we can do, in spite of all we can do, it is by the grace of God we are saved.

As our part of the gospel covenant, we agree to exercise saving faith in Christ—to trust in Him, lean upon Him, have full confidence in Him, rely totally upon Him. As extensions of that faith, we repent of our sins, are baptized, receive the Holy Spirit, and seek to cultivate that Spirit at all times. Thus repentance, baptism, and efforts to live a Christlike life are all fruits of my faith, expressions of my faith, manifestations of my faith. They are not works standing alone. Our belief is that the works of man are a necessary but an insufficient condition for salvation. My works indicate how serious I am taking my covenant with Christ. They can never, worlds without end, save me, but they are necessary in that they evidence the depth of my devotion to the Master. True faith always results in faithfulness.

I remember one time Greg asked me, while we were sitting in a restaurant and discussing grace and works: "Bob," he said, "the problem in Mormonism is that you have so many things to do to be saved." I said, "Like what?" "Well," he said, "you must go to Church, read scripture, pay tithing, be baptized, go to the temple, and on and on." It was a good reflective moment. I said to him, "Greg, do you ever read scripture?" And he answered...

GREG: "Yes, of course I read scripture."

BOB: "Why do you read scripture?" I followed up. And he said, "To feed my soul through entering the spirit of worship and devotion." I said, "You know, I think there was a time when I read scripture because President Spencer W. Kimball, the president of the Church, counseled the Latter-day Saints to read scripture every day. But that was over thirty years ago. Do you know why I read scripture now? To feed my soul and to worship." Let me say this in another way. I think there was a time I went to Church because I knew I was supposed to, but I don't do that anymore. I go to the Church now because I want to worship and I want to be with the Saints. I once paid my tithing because I felt under an obligation to do so, but I pay tithing now because I love God and want to express my love to him and my meager appreciation for all he has done for me and mine. When my heart is truly changed, my works will follow. The scriptures teach that we will be judged by our works. That message is sounded over and over in the New Testament and Book of Mormon. But I do not believe we will be saved by the merits of our works, but rather by the merits and mercy of the Holy Messiah; rather, our works will evidence the kind of people we have become, just what our trust in and reliance upon the Savior have done to transform our souls and our daily deeds.

GREG: We are in agreement, Bob, that good works are a by-product of true, saving faith in Christ.

BOB: Let me pose another question. If one reads the Acts of the Apostles carefully, it becomes extremely difficult, at least for Latter-day Saints, to understand how Protestants can conclude that the ordinances or sacraments, like baptism, are not necessary and thus how divine authority is not essential. Could you please comment on your notion of a "priesthood of all believers" and how exactly you see the sacraments of the church?

GREG: Since the question of spiritual authority is important to both Latter-day Saints and Evangelicals, it's not unusual to be asked questions about authority from my Mormon friends. Evangelical Christianity looks back to the days of the Protestant Reformation and Martin Luther's emphasis of the "priesthood of all believers" to affirm that all Christians possess authority to serve God. Understanding that one of Luther's grievances with the Catholic Church was that the church's structured priesthood prevented the laity from being empowered to serve God directly, he advocated a universal priesthood authority for all true believers in Jesus Christ. Supportive of this idea, the Apostle John writes in his greeting in Revelation that Jesus, "has made us to be a kingdom of priests to serve His God and Father (1:6)." So, for Evangelicals, we feel our authority does not come to us from the institution of a local church or even a denomination, but rather directly from Jesus Christ as a result of our salvation by His grace. Obviously, various Christian denominations differ on the role of their clergy and their laity, as to what function they may serve, but generally speaking it is understood that all Christians have the authority to serve God, to share His love with others, and to proclaim the Good News of Jesus.

I sometimes feel that my LDS friends are made uncomfortable with our lack of structured and credentialed authority. This is easy to understand when one recognizes the very detailed order of authority that exists within the organization of Mormonism, but I do feel the need to caution them with the thought that just because something is different doesn't make it wrong. In Mormonism, the offices of the Priesthood are defined by age and responsibility, and the emphasis on "holding the keys" and "having proper authority" is regularly taught. However, for Evangelicals the idea of needing to have an office or to be in a certain church or denomination seems unbiblical. We believe as an individual comes to saving faith in Jesus Christ that he is immediately imparted a spiritual gift (Ephesians 4 and I Corinthains 12) and encouraged to discover what their gift is and to use it to the glory of God. Again, while denominations might differ on who should appropriately baptize new converts or who should officiate over the Lord's table (the sacrament of the Lord's supper), we would not confuse this with the essence of authority, but rather a function or form of authority. For example, the New Testament does not say that new converts are to be baptized by the overseer or pastor, nor does it say that only bishops or clergy can administer communion. Evangelicals believe that the Bible teaches us that before Jesus Christ ascended to heaven He gave us His Great Commission Charge, and that in that charge Jesus told us to go into all the world to preach the Gospel of Jesus Christ and to make disciples of all nations knowing that He would be with us even unto the end of the age (Mt. 28:18-20). We Evangelicals believe that every believer has the right and the authority to serve God and administer His truth to everyone because Jesus Christ is with us and in us to advance His Kingdom here on earth.

Let's look at the other side of the coin. It seems to us that sometimes you folks seem to believe that baptism is what saves you. In addition, if you really believe that salvation comes through the Atonement of Christ, why do you build and attend temples and perform ordinances?

Bob: We believe baptism and what we call the "ordinances of salvation" are essential. The ordinances or sacraments are, as you might say, outward expressions of an inward covenant. They are visible rites that manifest an invisible covenant with Christ. But baptism does not save me. Confirmation does not save me. Ordination to the priesthood does not save me. The Sacrament of the Lord's Supper does not save me. The ordinances of the temple do not save me. Let me state this as clearly as I can: Jesus saves me! It is His atoning blood that saves me. While the ordinances point me to Him, remind me of Him, connect me to Him, they are but channels of His divine power. While we believe that the temple is the house of the Lord, it is not the Lord! The covenants and ordinances of the gospel, including those in the temple, are, for us, extensions of and manifestations of our faith in the Lord Jesus Christ. Again, the ordinances are necessary but not sufficient.

GREG: Let me ask a tough one. It seems to me that one of the great divides between us is the nature of God. Bob, tell us exactly what Latter-day Saints believe about God once being a man and also about how man may become as God. There are no doctrines in all of Mormonism that are more troubling to Evangelicals than these.

BOB: Latter-day Saints believe that God is in very deed our Heavenly Father, the Father of the spirits of all men and women. We believe He has a body of flesh and bones as tangible as man's, just as does His Beloved Son, Jesus Christ. We believe that the Father, Son, and Holy Spirit are three separate and distinct personages. We believe they are one in purpose, in attributes and powers, in mind and glory, indeed, that they are infinitely more one than they are separate. We believe the simplest reading of the New Testament reveals the members of the Godhead as truly separate and distinct. Joseph Smith taught that God is an Exalted Man, a Man of Holiness, and that while He is God and possesses every power, every divine quality, and every perfected attribute, He is not of a different species with mortal men and women. Now don't misunderstand me here: the chasm between man and God is immense, but we do not believe it is unbridgeable, nor do we hold the same Creator-creature dichotomy that most Christians do. For us God is a man, a person, an actual being with a glorified and exalted personality.

It is true that Presidents Joseph Smith and Lorenzo Snow both spoke of God once being a man, but we know very little if anything beyond that idea itself. I am not aware of any official statement or declaration of doctrine that goes beyond what I have just stated. Anything you may hear or read beyond that is speculative.

GREG: I appreciate your honesty. But what about the second part of my question: do you believe that men and women can one day become a god or god-dess?

Bob: We come to the earth to take a physical body, be schooled and gain experiences, and develop sweet and lasting relationships. We strive to keep the commandments and grow in faith and spiritual graces until we are prepared to go where God and Christ are. For Latter-day Saints, eternal life consists in being with God; in addition, it entails being like God. A study of Christian history reveals that the doctrine of the deification of man, the idea that human beings can, through the atoning sacrifice of Jesus Christ and through the divine transformation of human nature—become a joint heir or co-inheritor with Christ to all the Father has—was taught in the early Christian church, at least into the fifth century by such thinkers as Irenaus, Clement of Alexandria, Athanasius, and Augustine. Orthodox Christianity still holds to a doctrine of deification today. While these individuals and groups may not believe the same way Latter-day Saints do, it is clear that the idea was not foreign to the people of the early church.

All men and women, like Christ, are made in the image and likeness of God, and so we feel it is nei-ther robbery nor heresy for the children of God to aspire to be like God; like any parent, our Heavenly Father would want his children to become and be all that he is. We believe such biblical phrases as "be ye therefore perfect, even as your Father which is in heaven is perfect" (Matthew 5:48), or becoming "joint heirs with Christ" (Romans 8:17), or "partakers of the divine nature" (2 Peter 1:4), or having "the mind of Christ" (1 Corinthians 2:16), or "when he shall appear we shall be like him, for we shall see him as he is" (1 John 3:2) all point toward this grand ideal. No sane or studied Latter-day Saint believes he or she can work their way to godhood, but we believe that because of the atoning blood of Christ, and through the sanctifying power of the Holy Spirit, men and women may over time be refined, renewed, and reinstated to the family of God. Although Latter-day Saints believe that godhood comes through the receipt of eternal life, we do not believe we will ever unseat or oust either God the Father or Jesus Christ; those holy beings are and forever will be the Gods we worship. Even though we believe in the ultimate deification of man, I am unaware of any authoritative statement in LDS literature that suggests that we will ever worship any being other than the ones within the Godhead.

PART III
QUESTIONS FROM THE AUDIENCE

D URING THE LAST *decade we have been invited to present our dialogue over fifty times throughout the United States, as well as in Canada and England. We have made it our business not to script the dialogue, so as to remain as fresh and spontaneous as possible. At the end of each dialogue, we have turned the time to the audience for questions. The following are representative of questions that have been raised again and again.*

QUESTION: One of the reasons we sometimes conclude that Mormons are not Christian is because of some of your really unusual doctrines. For example, isn't it true that some of your church leaders taught that Adam is God?

BOB: I'm glad you asked that one early on, because it gives me the opportunity to make an important clarifying point regarding LDS doctrine. A few years ago, Greg was in my office one day. We were chatting about a number of things, including doctrine. He said to me, "Bob, Mormonism teaches some pretty strange doctrines!" "Like what?" I asked. "Oh, for example," he said, "you believe in blood atonement." I responded: "No we don't." "Yes you do," he came right back. "There are several statements by Brigham Young, Heber C. Kimball, and Jedediah Grant that teach such things." "I'm aware of those statements," I said, "*but they do not represent the doctrine of our Church.* We believe in the blood atonement of Jesus Christ, and that alone."

"What do you mean they don't represent the doctrine of your Church," Greg said. "They were spoken by major Church leaders." I explained that such statements were made, for the most part, during the time of the Mormon Reformation and they were examples of a kind of "revival rhetoric" in which the leaders of the Church were striving to "raise the bar" in terms of obedience and faithfulness. Then he said: "Bob, many of my fellow Christians have noted how hard it is to figure out what Mormons believe. They say it's like trying to nail Jell-o to the wall! What do you people believe? How do you decide what is your doctrine and what is not?" It was at this point that I sensed that we were in the midst of a very important conversation, one that was pushing me to the limits and requiring that I do some of the deepest thinking I had done for a long time. His questions were valid. They were in no way mean-spirited. They were not intended to entrap or embarrass me or the Church. He simply was asking for information.

I suggested that he consider the following three ideas:

1. The "doctrine of the Church" today has a rather narrow focus and direction; central and saving doctrines are what we are called upon to emphasize, not tangential and peripheral teachings.

2. Not everything that was ever spoken or written by a Church leader in the past is necessarily a part of the doctrine of the Church today.

3. In determining whether something is a part of the doctrine of the Church, we might ask: Is it found within the four standard works, within the Bible, the Book of Mormon, the Doctrine and Covenants, and the Pearl of Great Price? Is it found within official declarations or proclamations? In the general

handbooks or approved curriculum of the Church today? Is it discussed in general conference or other official gatherings by leaders today?

It is worth noting that most anti-Mormonism focuses on statements by Church leaders of the past that deal with peripheral or non-central issues. No one criticizes us for a belief in God; in the divinity of Jesus Christ or his atoning work; in the literal bodily resurrection of Christ and the eventual resurrection of mankind; in baptism by immersion; in the gift of the Holy Ghost; the sacrament of the Lord's Supper, etc. But we are attacked regularly for statements in our literature on such matters as the following:

+ God's life before he was God;
+ how Jesus was conceived;
+ teachings about Adam as God;
+ details concerning what it means to become like God hereafter;
+ why Blacks were denied the priesthood prior to 1978, etc.

While we love the scriptures and thank God regularly for them, we do not worship the scriptures. Nor do we believe in what many in the Christian world call "scriptural inerrancy." We believe, for example, that one can have sufficient confidence and even reverence for holy writ without believing that every word between Genesis 1:1 and Revelation 22:21 is the word-for-word dictation of the Almighty or that the Bible now reads as it has always read. In like manner, we can sustain with all our hearts the prophets and apostles without believing that they are perfect or that everything they say or do is exactly what God wants said and done. In the same way that we do not believe in scriptural inerrancy, we do not believe in apostolic or prophetic infallibility. Moses made mistakes, but we love and sustain him and his writings nonetheless. Peter made mistakes, but we still honor him and study his words. Paul made mistakes, but we admire his boldness and dedication and treasure his epistles. James pointed out that Elijah "was a man subject to like passions as we are" (James 5:17), and Joseph Smith taught that "a prophet [is] a prophet only when he [is] acting as such."

So I suppose I'm suggesting this: Surely you and I will encounter theological differences between our faith traditions, some differences that may appear to be almost insurmountable. That is to say, we will disagree on certain matters, just as you might disagree with another Evangelical who has a differing view from you on the ordination of women or the manner of baptism or the gift of tongues. If we're going to disagree, however, let's disagree on the right stuff, on matters that we actually believe and teach today, not just something that was said years ago but is not really a part of the doctrine of the Church. If you're going to analyze The Church of Jesus Christ of Latter-day Saints, spend your time studying what the Church has become, what it is today, in the 21st century. Does that make sense?

GREG: Do you folks hear what Bob is saying? I think what he has just said is very important, because it can help us to be honest and accurate and forthright in our conversations, in addressing the genuine differences between us. I think it is both important and fair to let Latter-day Saints define themselves and not to obligate them to believe and defend everything that might have been taught in their 180-year history.

QUESTION: Why do the Latter-day Saints seem to be suddenly stressing so much their belief in Christ and grace, when these things weren't much talked about some years ago? Is it to build up your public image or to slip into mainstream Christianity?

Bob: That's a good question, one that we're asked quite often lately. First of all, I would state categorically (and I mean no offense by this statement), The Church of Jesus Christ of Latter-day Saints has no desire to move into the mainstream of Christianity. We are what we are and we believe what we believe. We profess to be "Christian, but different." Those differences—such as our belief in an apostasy or falling away; the need for a restoration through a modern prophet, Joseph Smith; the fact that priesthood or divine authority was restored by heavenly messengers; the historical veracity and doctrinal truthfulness of the Book of Mormon and other modern scripture; the doctrine of the premortal existence of man; the place of temples, eternal marriage and family, etc.—these ideas set us apart from many other Christians. But we feel strongly that our strength lies in our distinctiveness, in what we have to offer the world. People are not joining our Church in ever-increasing numbers nowadays because we are just like the Catholics or Methodists or Lutherans down the street. There's definitely something different about the Mormons.

Now, while we have no desire to slip quietly into the mainstream, we do not, at the same time, want people to misunderstand who we are and what we believe. A blatant statement that "Mormons aren't Christian" can be terribly misleading. Does it mean that we do not believe there ever was a man named Jesus of Nazareth? Does it mean that we do not accept or read or believe in the New Testament? Does it mean that we do not accept the virgin birth, teachings, miracles, suffering, death, atonement, and resurrection of Jesus, as set forth in the New Testament? Do we not believe that Jesus was sin-less and lived a perfect life and that we should strive to live as He lived? If anyone hears that Latter-day Saints are not Christian and assumes that declara-tion means any of the above, then serious injustice and misrepresentation have been perpetrated. And so one major reason why you are hearing the Latter-day Saints stress their Christianity more than ever before is because there are so many people out there crying out that we are not Christian.

Let me get personal about this. I love Jesus Christ. He is my Savior and Redeemer, my only hope for peace here and eternal life hereafter. He is my Lord, my God, and my King. I have given my life to Him, have submitted and surrendered my will to Him, and my faith, my trust, my confidence, my complete reliance is upon Him and in His atoning blood. I don't know how to say that more clearly. I worship the Christ of the New Testament. Now, do I believe some additional things about Jesus, things that have been made known through additional scripture or latter-day prophets? Yes, of course. But supplementation is not the same as contradiction. The Gospel of John teaches us much more about the ministry of the risen Lord on the shore of the Sea of Galilee than the Synoptics, but John is not contradicting his evangelistic colleagues.

One other reason you are hearing more about Christ from the Latter-day Saints is because over the last few decades we have become more scripturally literate. We know our Bibles better today than we ever have. In addition, through the repetitive emphasis placed by President Ezra Taft Benson, the Mormons are more conversant with the teachings of the Book of Mormon. The Book of Mormon has a high Christology; it is filled with what might be called "redemptive theology." Whether one accepts the historicity of the Book of Mormon or not, the casual Christian reader of the Book of Mormon would have to admit that it teaches over and over of the need for men and women to acknowledge their fallen state, come unto Christ through faith and repentance, and be reborn through the Atonement and the cleansing ministry of the Holy Spirit.

QUESTION: Pastor Johnson, don't you feel you are being too kind to Dr. Millet and the Mormons? Wouldn't you help him more if you were more confrontive about his false beliefs?

GREG: The point I'm trying to make is that Bob Millet is not my enemy. I repeat: he's not my enemy. Nor am I Bob Millet's enemy. And even if Bob were my enemy, I have been instructed by Jesus to pray for my enemies. We have enemies out there, to be sure. Satan is the arch-enemy. Immorality and indecency and abuse and brutality—these are our enemies. And we both agree on that. And so, I don't feel the need to debate him, put him down, embarrass him, because this is not the heart of Jesus. A confrontational approach to spiritual conversations is not in any way more Godly or effective, in my opinion, and I believe 1 Peter 3:15 reminds us of the need to answer correctly, but to do so with gentleness and respect. Having said this, however, I do believe that I have asked and continue to ask Bob, both in private and during our public dialogues, some very difficult questions about the nature of God, the place of Grace in Christian salvation, the Mormon concept of apostasy and restoration, the person of Joseph Smith and his credibility as a prophet, and about the historicity of the Book of Mormon among other things. I don't think I'm any less hard on Mormon doctrine than I have ever been, I just think the foundation of relationship is the best way to talk about important matters of theology.

QUESTION: How do Mormons feel about other churches? Since you believe there was an apostasy or falling away, do you even believe we're Christian?

BOB: Latter-day Saints believe that truth is to be found throughout the earth—among men and women in all walks of life, among sages and philosophers, and among people of differing religious persuasions. But they do claim that through the call of Joseph Smith and his successors, and through the establishment of The Church of Jesus Christ of Latter-day Saints, the fullness of the gospel of Jesus Christ has been restored to earth. They value the truths had among the children of God everywhere but believe that theirs is the "only true church" in the sense that the same divine authority and the same doctrines of salvation had from the beginning are now found in their fullness in the LDS faith. Our definition of Christian is broad: we believe that any person who professes a belief in the divinity of Jesus and confesses Him as Lord and Savior is a Christian. As

Greg said earlier, no one of us is in a position to look into other people's hearts and to know their true relationship with God or with Christ.

QUESTION: Do you pray together?

GREG: I would have to admit that as an Evangelical Christian there are some facets of Mormon thought, particularly as they relate to the nature of God, that concern me. You might be asking the question: If Bob is praying to his God, and you're praying to your God, are you really praying to the same God? While we have our differences on the Trinity or the corporeality of God, we have chosen to kind of set that aside. In the sincerity of our friendship and the authenticity of our relationship, when we're together and have a meal, for example, Bob might ask if he can bless the meal, and I am more than willing that he do so. On other occasions I will offer the prayer. In June 2001 Bob had a very serious heart attack. We almost lost him a few years ago. His heart stopped and it was necessary to pull out the paddles and re-start the heart. And I'm so glad that the Lord said, "Not yet."

Four months later we traveled to Boston together. On that trip, Bob had a few more heart troubles. We struggled with it all day long and finally, against his insistence that we not do so, I stated, "We are going to the hospital." We checked him in, and he was evaluated very carefully. And at about 11:30 at night, I said, "Bob, I think you know, personally, that I pray for you. But I was wondering, under the circumstances, whether you would feel comfortable allowing me to pray over you, for your full recovery." It was a very special moment for us and I remember Bob said, "Yes, I would really like you to do that." I prayed for him, and then something happened that I was not at all offended by. He said, "You know, Greg, I really appreciate that prayer, and the fact that you initiated that prayer causes me to also realize that it would be appropriate in a time like this to ask members of the priesthood to come and administer to me, to anoint me with oil and give me a blessing. This is not that I don't accept your prayer, for I appreciated it very much." I said, "I'd be happy to call them." And we were able to contact those men, and they came, and they left, and I thought that was really an interesting experience, relating very specifically to the topic of prayer. As Mormons and Evangelicals we obviously both believe in the idea of prayer and, as I've already said, over meals and perhaps to begin or close a group meeting, we have allowed each other to pray and to pray before one another knowing that we are indeed praying to two very different concepts of God. As a result of this, Bob and I have never communed in prayer together or engaged in extended personal prayer with one another.

QUESTION: Bob, what are some things that you feel affirm the truthfulness of the Book of Mormon? I might not agree with what you say but would be interested in your response.

BOB: Some of the things that Latter-day Saint scholars have published have addressed what might be called external and, more especially, internal evidences of the Book of Mormon, such matters as its literary structure, its Hebraic patterns, and other things that point toward its antiquity. Years ago Professor Richard Bushman published a very significant article on the Book of Mormon and the American Revolution. He commented on the fact that Alexander Campbell, who was probably one of the very first critics of the Book of Mormon, had observed that the Book of Mormon simply responded to nineteenth-century issues and thus reflected nineteenth-century thinking. Richard very astutely pointed out that there's nothing in the Book of Mormon to suggest, for example, the spirit of revolution or rebellion. Thus when you read early in 1

Nephi 13 of a description of the revolutionary war, there's no concept there of revolution, no notion of the colonists revolting against the British. Rather what you see is the spirit of deliverance, a message that makes its way throughout the Old Testament. Moses didn't lead Israel out of Egypt through a major revolt; instead, ancient Israel was delivered from bondage. Well, that's one of many kinds of things that have been published.

Now, if you were to push me regarding archeological evidences, that's another matter. I don't know much about that, and I don't have much to say about that. But I would make this observation: archeological evidences represent something, as far as I'm concerned, that are yet to come. It's just been within the last couple of decades that, archeologically speaking, we've come to know through external evidence that there really was an Abraham. Now, obviously most of us believed in Abraham long before we discovered archeological evidence for him. Where is the tangible evidence, beyond the text itself, for vital New Testament moments—for the feeding of 5,000, for the healing of the man born blind, for the resurrection of Jesus, etc.? Some things we know because we have an inner spiritual witness of their truthfulness. Tangible evidence can fan the flame of one's witness, but much that we accept about the life and ministry of our Lord and Savior we accept on faith. I believe strongly that our faith in something as critical as the resurrection of Christ is dependent upon an actual historical event, a key moment in time. I feel exactly the same way about the Book of Mormon. For me, its greatest evidence is to be found in the power of its message. I can exercise faith in the unseen for the time being and wait until archaeological evidences catch up with us.

QUESTION: Rev. Johnson, if God is not progressive, what does He do?

GREG: This question usually comes in various expressions but seems always to deal with the essence of God's completeness. To put the question in common thought, "What does God do all the time? Is He just sitting around listening to harp music while lounging around on the clouds?" I think this question comes because in Mormonism there is a great emphasis on what Latter-day Saints call "eternal progression." When a Latter-day Saint hears me say that God is completely perfect, completely fulfilled, and in need of nothing, they sometimes think I believe in a very static God, a kind of bored deity who has arrived and has nothing new to learn or experience. To Evangelicals, however, the idea that God has more to learn or can become more than He is, is unbiblical. I remember when Bob and I were presenting our dialogue at Utah State University that a young man asked me this kind of question. I did my best to explain God's nature and that He receives glory and worship from His creation but that He was not in any way dependant upon it for His happiness, since He is and has always been completely, perfectly, God. As I concluded, I sensed the young man was somewhat unimpressed with my answer and my description of God's being. Then Bob spoke up and said that he appreciated the Evangelicals' ability to do "awe." Bob continued by saying that LDS people could learn much from the Evangelical focus on worship and awe, as LDS theology is quite often very practical. The idea of God being completely worthy and awesome and that He deserves to receive constant worship and adoration was something Bob felt he had gained an appreciation of as he had learned more about Evangelicals. He felt that Evangelical worship and praise was something that Mormons could gain insight and inspiration from. Well, needless to say, what Bob said to this young man had a much deeper impact than my words did, and I thought it was a good example of how we both help each other's constituents understand our religious other.

QUESTION: How can God be three Gods and one at the same time? In other words, how do you explain the concept of the Trinity?

GREG: Somehow this question always surfaces as the most difficult theological difference Mormons have with Evangelical/Protestant Christians. Acknowledging that comprehensive works have attempted to explore the essence of the Trinitarian nature of God, let me attempt to give the quick "man on the street" response. Evangelicals and all three branches of historic Christendom (Catholic, Orthodox, and Protestant) affirm that God is uniquely one and three simultaneously. We believe that the Old and New Testaments teach there is only one true God. The *Shema* states, "Hear oh Israel, the Lord our God, the Lord is one" (Deuteronomy 6:4), and Isaiah says, "before me there was no god formed, nor will there be one after me...apart from me there is no savior" (Isaiah 43:10). And yet, any reader of the New Testament would clearly see that three are identified as God: the Father, the Son, and the Holy Spirit. The question naturally arises, then, Are there three Gods or is there only one God? Christians through the ages have affirmed the oneness and threeness of God in response to the plain reading of the text of scripture.

Clearly, the Old Testament teaches us there is one and only one God, as the Jewish faith continues to affirm; this is why they have rejected Jesus Christ as being God. As well, the New Testament tells us there are three persons in the Godhead, and yet Jesus says, "I and the Father are one" (John. 10:30). Therefore, with the early church Fathers at Nicea, Evangelical Christians affirm that God is one being, not just one in purpose, but one ontological being that mysteriously possesses three distinct personalities at the same time, meaning that the Father, the Son, and the Holy Spirit co-exist and have so for all eternity. The baptism of Jesus is often put forward as a challenge to the doctrine of the Trinity, as one would note the presence of the Son in the Jordan River, the voice of the Father speaking from Heaven, and the Spirit descending like a dove. While most Evangelicals struggle to fully explain how God can be three and yet one at the same time, we feel it is not problematic, that our finite minds are incapable of knowing the infinite mind and being of God. As we acknowledge this however, we do not believe that the Trinity is contradictory or illogical and that in fact it is the best way to interpret the Bible and understand the nature of God.

Question: I want to follow up on that question with Bob. Do you believe Jesus Christ is eternally God? How do you understand John 1:1?

Bob: It's interesting that the title page of the Book of Mormon states that one of the major purposes of the book is to prove that "Jesus is the Christ, the ETERNAL GOD." In the book itself Christ is given such titles as the Almighty, Almighty God, Eternal Father, Eternal God, Everlasting Father, Everlasting God, Father of heaven and of earth, God of Abraham, and Isaac, and Jacob, King of heaven, Lord God Almighty, Lord God Omnipotent, Most High God, Son of the Eternal Father, Son of the Everlasting God, and the Supreme Being. There's no question about it: Jesus Christ is God! And if it were not so, he could not save us.

Now, to be sure, Latter-day Saints believe in a premortal existence and that Jesus became, under the direction of the Father, the Creator of worlds and was in fact the God of the ancients, the Deity to whom Enoch, Noah, Abraham, Isaac, Jacob, Joseph, Samuel, Moses, Isaiah and the prophets looked for direction and eternal deliverance. We believe there

is no contradiction between the following two sen-
tences: (1) Jesus Christ was not always God; and (2)
Jesus Christ is the Eternal God. For one thing, the
words translated as *eternal,* in both Hebrew (*olam*)
and Greek (*aeon*) seem originally to have referred to
such ideas as "long duration," the period from antiquity to futurity, indefinite futurity, continuous
existence, an age, an epoch, relative time, prolonged
time. In fact, the earliest connotations of the Hebrew
word olam were "hidden or distant time belonging
to the remote and inscrutable past or future from
the standpoint of the present." (See Brown, Driver,
Briggs, *A Hebrew and English Lexicon of the Old
Testament;* Kittel, *Theological Dictionary of the New
Testament.*) While I personally do not agree with
the Openness theologians in regard to what God
knows about the future—I believe the scriptures
clearly teach that He knows all things; the Book of
Mormon states that "there is nothing save He knows
it"—I agree wholeheartedly with their assessment
that the classical model of God as being *immutable*
(unchangeable), *impassible* (without passions, unable
to be moved by his children), and, especially, *timeless*
are neo-Platonic notions that are at odds with the
God of the Old and New Testaments.

To clarify, the Latter-day Saints believe in the three members of the Godhead—the Father, Son, and Holy Spirit. We believe they are three distinct personages, three Beings, three separate Gods. We are not, however, polytheistic. We believe the doctrine of the Trinity, as taught throughout Christendom today, reflects more of the decisions of post-New Testament church councils than the teachings of the New Testament itself. Now to be sure, the scriptures, including Latter-day Saint scriptures, teach that the members of the Godhead are one; in fact, we believe they are infinitely more one than they are separate. Each is God. Each possesses all of the attributes of Godliness. They are completely and totally united, thus constituting a divine community that is often referred to simply as "God" (2 Nephi 31:21; Alma 11:44; 3 Nephi 11:36; D&C 20:28).

John wrote that "In the beginning was the Word, and the Word was with God, and the Word was God. The same was in the beginning with God." (John 1:1-2.) From an LDS perspective, these verses mean the following: In the premortal existence, Christ, designated here as the Word, existed. He was with God, meaning with God the Father. Further, the Word (Jesus Christ), was God. God the Father existed in an earlier realm, as did God the Son. In other words, Jesus held the powers of Godhood in the First Estate, just as did his Eternal Father. Two prominent Church leaders and doctrinal writers, Joseph Fielding Smith and Bruce R. McConkie, have suggested that to say that Christ is eternal or from everlasting to everlasting is to say that he is from one premortal existence to the next. In the words of a Book of Mormon prophet, "the course of the Lord is one eternal round."

QUESTION: Why are there no crosses in or upon LDS churches? Someone told me that Mormons do not believe that Jesus died on the cross for their sins.

BOB: Many early Latter-day Saints came from the Puritan tradition, which opposed ceremonialism, including the use of crosses. If my memory holds correctly, in its early years, Baptists did not use crosses until they became more mainstream Protestant in nature (until the 1830s). Latter-day Saints believe that Jesus' suffering in the Garden of Gethsemane was redemptive and that what went on during those hours of suffering was a significant part of His atonement. For this reason, it is not uncommon to hear either Latter-day Saints or persons describing LDS doctrine suggesting that the atonement took place only in Gethsemane. This is not correct. We believe that what began in Gethsemane was completed on the cross, and that Jesus' suffering and death on the cross are a vital part of His overall atoning mission. Thus it is not unusual to find references in the Book of Mormon or in latter-day prophets' speeches that mention Jesus dying on the cross for our sins.

We are neither turned off nor offended by crosses, whether they be on necklaces, ministerial clothing, or church buildings. In a very broad sense, the cross was Paul's symbol of the atoning sacrifice of Jesus Christ. How could we be opposed to that? While we look to Gethsemane and Golgotha in our study of and deep appreciation for what the Savior has done for us, we rejoice also in the events that took place in the Garden Tomb—namely, Christ's rise from the dead. In short, we celebrate the living Christ.

QUESTION: I've been told that while the visible LDS church is made up of a happy and respectable bunch there is a private version of Mormonism that is much more sinister and suspect. Would you comment on this?

BOB: The only way I know how to answer this question is in a personal way. I've been LDS all my life. I was raised as a Latter-day Saint in Louisiana and, as I mentioned earlier, most of my friends were of other faiths. I have since lived in New York, New Jersey, Massachusetts, Connecticut, Idaho, Florida, Georgia, and Utah, and I have been intimately involved in the work of the Church through the years. Since 1973 I've been employed by the Church as a marriage and family counselor, religious instructor and professor, and university administrator. I've seen the Church from all sides—from right to left, and from top to bottom. I've worked closely with rank and file members and with church leaders at all levels of administration. In all that time I have never encountered but one brand of Mormonism—the public version. I'm not sure where the secret brand—the one advertised by our critics as scheming, mischievous, power-hungry, occultish, and dark—is to be found but I haven't come across it. I think I could say that what you see is what you get.

QUESTION: Why do Latter-day Saints waste their time sending missionaries to people who are already Christian?

BOB: Because we believe what we have to share with others represents a fullness of the gospel, and that the fullness is not found elsewhere. We feel a responsibility, in the spirit of our Lord's Great

Commission, to make the message available to all who will hear. We essentially say to people of other Christian faiths: "We haven't come to take away any truth that you already possess or to find fault with you. Keep the good you have and let us see if we can add to it." Those who are content with what they have are perfectly free to express that to the LDS missionaries. Those who are curious, unsatisfied with their present faith or way of life or those who may be seeking for answers to some of life's puzzling questions, may find an encounter with the Mormons worth their time.

QUESTION: Greg, I was just wondering what your greatest frustration or worry with Evangelicalism might be. Bob, let me pose the same question to you about Mormonism.

GREG: We're told in Joseph Smith's story that he went into a grove to pray, to determine which church he should join. He says in his official history that there was a good deal of confusion where he lived and many competing voices of Christianity during that time. I'm not sure that a great deal of improvement has taken place since that time. While I appreciate the heart of Evangelicals to be an expression of vibrant and united Christianity, there is still far too much division in the Body of Christ in our world today. My heart is often heavy about this matter. Evangelicals need to demonstrate more effectively that we are truly committed to the call of Jesus to be one in Him.

Bob: It's almost inevitable that with continued church growth there comes a kind of institutionalization, a rigidity, and a rule-driven way of doing things that you would like very much to avoid. There is a spiritual spontaneity that you would like to maintain, the kind that was had in the early Christian Church and in the early days of Joseph Smith. One of my concerns is the growing complexity of the Church, the tendency of some local leaders to try to overstructure the lives of the Saints in terms of programs, policies, and procedures. I would much rather see us focus more upon teaching the gospel more effectively on Sunday, visiting our people and letting them know we care about them, and then allowing them some time during the week to do what we taught them on Sunday. We need to focus more attention on becoming and being, not just doing. I fear a kind of regimented, sterile, institutionalization, rather than maintaining a spiritual spontaneity that for many is so very attractive today and made the church very attractive in the nineteenth century.

GREG: One more comment, if I might. I believe the Bible tells us there will be both Calvinists and Arminians in heaven, Charismatics and non-charismatics there, blacks and whites and browns and reds and yellows. Those who are high church, and those who are low church. But we as Evangelicals have allowed ourselves to hide behind denominational walls and to convey a disunity that saddens me. And as I look at the church in Utah, and around the country, I long to see a kind of unity that Jesus prayed for in the last night of His life: that the believers would be one, so that the world would know the Father had sent the Son. When someone needs a pastor and turns to the yellow pages of the phone directory, does he call the Baptists, the Presbyterians, the Lutherans, the Evangelical Free, or perhaps a Pentecostal Church? One man, finding himself in this plight, said to me: "I don't know who to call, and so I just close the book." Paul explained to the Corinthians that the body is made up of many parts, and so we're not going to eradicate denominationalism nor bring to an end the reality of many different nuances of Christian faith in our time. But I sure would like to see a Christianity in America, and around the world today, that is working harder to achieve one Lord, one faith, one baptism (Ephesians 4:5).

QUESTION: Pastor Johnson, do you think Mormons can be "saved Christians" in the same way that a person who attends a revival is saved by accepting Jesus as Savior and Lord?

GREG: This is an excellent question that is actually asking two things at the same time. (1): Is Mormonism Christian, in the orthodox sense of the word? and (2) Can individual Mormons be saved Christians? Perhaps the safest thing to say about an individual's salvation is that we can never be completely sure. I don't mean this as a copout, but only God knows the heart of an individual, and so for us to say who is and who is not saved is a position we should not and cannot take, a judgment we are not in a position to render. If you were to ask me if my friend Bob Millet is a saved Christian, I would have to answer that I do not know for sure. But I can say that it is entirely possible that he and other Mormons could be saved Christians in that they have a sincere and genuine relationship with Jesus Christ. Now, before you get nervous and suppose that I am heretical, there are fundamental doctrines of Mormonism that I see as inconsistent with historic orthodox or biblical Christianity.

I would not say that the differences between our two faith traditions are minimal. They are not. As an Evangelical I would not encourage a person who claims to be a Mormon Christian to remain where they are; if I had my way, as we suggested earlier, Bob Millet would embrace the Evangelical faith. But Christianity is, above and beyond everything else, all about relationships, particularly one's relationship with Jesus Christ. And only God and the individual can know about that. So to be specific to your question, it is conceivable to me that a Mormon could be as saved as someone who got saved at a revival meeting, because ultimately I cannot truly know anyone's heart, but I would be very cautious in saying this because enough of traditional Mormon doctrine as I was taught it and understand it is not consistent with what we call Christian orthodoxy.

One last thing: I find more and more that a quick and easy label does not often serve us well. By asking the question you did, did you assume that everyone who goes forward at a revival meeting truly gets saved? Of course not; there are plenty of people who "get saved" who are no more saved than a pagan. I say: Let's keep talking about Jesus with one another: Who is He to us? What did He do for us? Is He God, and how is He eternal and divine, while at the same time human and limited by His incarnation? If we will do the hard work of getting beyond the easy labeling of a person, we will learn some pretty amazing things and the conversation will have greater influence in all of our lives. This is a very important point for me. Bob and I talk regularly about "conversation stoppers" and "conversation starters." A genuine, honest question, posed with respect and kindness is a conversation starter.

QUESTION: Greg, if Robert died suddenly, would he (according to your beliefs) go to hell because he is not Evangelical? Bob, do you think your friendship will end at death?

GREG: This question is quite similar to the one just asked, but let me add one more thing. I can remember a long time ago having a conversation with a Latter-day Saint where it suddenly dawned on both of us that the idea of one of us being "right" and the other person being "wrong" was really no victory for either of us. If we can imagine ourselves walking on a road, taking a long journey together, neither of us would be happy if the other one could not reach the final destination. Each of us might be happy that we made it but sad that our friend did not. Therefore the question you ask can never be answered in the spirit of "I'm right and you're wrong" or "I'm going to heaven while you're bound for hell," but rather that we both long to go to heaven together and must be willing to do whatever it would take to help each other discover the Truth. Bob, what do you think?

Bob: Latter-day Saints believe that at the time of death our spirits, our true identities, continue to live until the time of the resurrection. We believe that relationships are among the most treasured of all earthly blessings and that such relationships are not intended to be dissolved at death. As a Mormon, I have a great hope of being with my wife and family forever, but then for me heaven would not really be heaven without the continued association of dear and valued friends. From our doctrinal perspective—and I promise that I am not trying here to skirt a sensitive issue—our Father in heaven is an omni-loving Deity and will grant to every man and women the light and truth and spiritual gifts and understanding that they seek. Thus, speaking from my own limited perspective, I fully intend to see Greg Johnson hereafter, if we don't first become sick of one another in this life!

QUESTION: For both of you: Where do Muslims, Buddhists, etc, fit under your umbrella?

GREG: I think Bob and I would respond similarly to your question. At the very least, as two who profess to be Christians, we would hold to absolute truth and the exclusivity of Jesus Christ as the only Way to salvation. Thus while we respect noble people from various world religions and appreciate the fact that there is much truth throughout the world, we are both persuaded that Christianity is God's unique truth and that Jesus Christ is the only way to make it to heaven.

BOB: I agree wholeheartedly, adding only the LDS distinctive that every man and woman will have the opportunity to learn of Christ and His gospel, either here or hereafter.

QUESTION: I have a couple of ways I want to phrase my question. First, how could God reveal to Greg Johnson one thing and to Bob Millet another? Or putting this another way, is it, within your respective systems of belief, possible that Greg Johnson is where God wants him to be and Bob Millet is where God wants him to be?

GREG: Ah yes—what we have here is the great question of God's revelation of truth and why He doesn't make clearer to everyone what that truth is. Let me illustrate. Because of the opportunities I have had with people like Bob Millet, other BYU religion faculty members, even some of the general authorities of the LDS Church, and various Mormons that I have talked with have asked me how it is that I have not converted to the LDS faith. A few years ago Bob and I were in Manchester, England. While there I was invited to share briefly, in various Mormon firesides, about my love for Jesus Christ, which I was happy to do. Later in the week, in meeting with a number of the LDS Church Educational System personnel in the UK, a lovely, silver-haired older woman approached me with tears in her eyes. She immediately confessed her need to apologize to me for the negative feelings she had felt toward me since the night I had spoken at one of the firesides. She wondered how I could have spent so much time with "Brother Millet" and even with general authorities and still not have embraced Mormonism. It was confusing to her how that could be. She had concluded that I must be a proud and arrogant young American pastor who could not recognize the truth. But upon listening as I spoke to this particular group, she had heard me, felt my heart, and sensed that my love for the Lord was genuine and that I was truly serving Jesus Christ with my life.

What happened to this dear lady is that she realized that her view of God's truth was too narrow and that God was working outside of the parameters she had set up. The converse of this is, however, true. One might well ask, "How is it that Bob Millet can visit with Evangelical leaders and scholars and not, at some point, be persuaded to leave Mormonism? I've been with the LDS best, he's been with the Evangelical best, and neither one of us has moved out of our respective traditions. It would be wrong to assume that neither Bob nor I are generally seeking truth and would be willing to embrace it wherever it might be found. I'm open to say that if God showed me that Mormonism was true that I'd become a Mormon. If God showed Bob that Evangelicalism was the right path, Bob would take that path. So this is really a dilemma. I ask myself: Why hasn't God made this matter clear? Clearly this question can be asked in the larger sense that people all over the world believe very different things about

God and the nature of Truth. The Bible says that there are those who "have a zeal but not according to truth (Romans 10:2)," so we need more than sincerity to call something Truth: Truth by definition is True. So, I continue to pray that Bob will discover all Truth God would have him discover. In the end I know that God would have us continue to build relationships, love one another, reason with one another, seek Him with all our hearts, and leave the results to Him and to the power of His Holy Spirit. This is what we're trying our best to do.

Bob: Let me utter an "Amen" to what Greg has said above. Let me be foolish enough to engage the issue of each of us being where God would have us be. An overly simplistic perspective on this would have God revealing the same thing to everyone and everyone joining the same church or adhering to the same doctrines. Oh, that life were that simple or that truth came to all in such a neat package! Obviously I believe 100% in what I am doing as a Latter-day Saint professor of religion at the Church's largest university. But I feel it is small-minded to suggest that Greg Johnson has not been involved seriously in moving the work of the Lord forward because I happen to still be a staunch Latter-day Saint. Likewise,

I would not be honest if I did not state forthrightly that I feel the moving hand of the Almighty in what I am doing, and yet Greg Johnson is still an Evangelical. Let me be more blunt. From my perspective— and I believe it is true and doctrinally sound—just because Greg hasn't been baptized as a Latter-day Saint (we would say, by one having proper authority) doesn't mean that he isn't just where he ought to be right now. Ultimately we serve each other best by committing to a very simple prayer—that God would lead and direct each of us to be and become all that He would have us be and become.

QUESTION: Dr. Millet, what do you two do when you are up against the wall, when you are face to face with an issue or a doctrine about which you simply cannot agree?

BOB: To some extent we've addressed ourselves to that question, but let's respond a little differently. I have, as I assume many of you do, a number of questions—doctrinal or historical—about my own faith tradition that I have not resolved or found adequate answers for. After I have taken the time to read, study, and research an issue and fill in whatever blanks I can, I put the question "on the shelf" and move on. As time passes, as new insights come, I am able to take many of those issues down from the shelf, for now they are no longer a problem for me. But I determined years ago that I would not obsess over or become unwound spiritually by the things that have neither been revealed nor discovered. I will not allow myself to throw the baby out with the bathwater. There are too many things I know for sure to allow myself to stumble over what I do not know, what I am still seeking information on. Greg and I have likewise chosen not to push too vigorously the hard buttons, to focus unduly on matters that divide us most directly. If, for example, we had chosen early in the process to cease our interactions because of our differences on the nature of God, we would have robbed ourselves of the requisite insight and relationship that came with time and experience, knowledge that allows us now to discuss this matter dispassionately and to come to some points of agreement that we would never have recognized a decade ago. There are elements of discipline and patience required to engage hard issues, a kind of awareness that borders on faith and trust that the Almighty will bring us into appropriate conversation on the tough matters when the time is right. As we have already stressed, these kinds of things cannot be hurried.

QUESTION: Why do Protestants look forward so passionately to the Rapture of the saints, while Mormons seldom discuss it?

BOB: Latter-day Saints look forward to the Second Coming of Christ in glory as much as any people. We believe fully that the Millennium will be initiated by power, Christ's power, and that our Master will then rule and reign for a thousand years as King of kings and Lord of lords. I for one cannot tell you how anxious I am to live in a world where lying and deceit and corruption have no place. We believe, as Paul taught the Thessalonians, that the righteous will be caught up to meet Christ in the clouds at the time of His coming. We do believe that there will be a period of great tribulation before Christ's return in glory to the world. At the same time, and while many LDS books have been written about the signs of the times and the need for proper preparation, there is a concern that the Latter-day Saints not become either eschatomanic or eschatophobic—caught up in an unhealthy and imbalanced manner with the end times, argumentative about the meanings of horns and beasts and numbers, or frightened to death by the whole thing and thus fearful of even discussing it. While we take seriously the parables of preparation in Matthew 25—particularly the parable of the ten virgins—we focus on provident living and daily spirituality, how best to prepare for that great and dreadful day.

QUESTION: What do Evangelicals think about the Word of Wisdom, the LDS health code? Do you have a similar code?

GREG: As I'm sure Bob will allude to at the close of this work, there is a phrase from Bishop Krister Stendahl that we have come to use quite often. It is called the princpile of "holy envy." Speaking broadly, I think most Evangelicals would feel very positively about the LDS Word of Wisdom teaching. And while we do not have as specific a code as the Latter-day Saints, we affirm the importance of the human body as the temple of the Holy Spirit. So living a life that would in some way harm our body such as smoking, excessive drinking, overeating, or the abuse of drugs, would be activities that are generally discouraged. Frankly, I appreciate the structure of the Word of Wisdom and wish that we Evangelicals were more determined to live healthier lives. Let me at the same time balance my thoughts. Paul spends much time in the New Testament encouraging us not to confuse spirituality with external practices;

one can dot all the i's and cross all the t's and remain unspiritual. He writes of this in regard to meats offered to idols and the observance of holy days and reminds us that in the end the condition of our heart is more important than a life dedicated to rule-keeping. As Christians we are told that we have liberty in all things; such liberty will allow Christians to disagree honestly on such an issue as drinking alcohol, for example. But to be sure, a good Christian testimony should reveal a healthy lifestyle.

QUESTION: You both advocate the need for greater understanding and friendship between persons of different faiths. Do you draw the line at marriage?

BOB: In all honesty, we would both draw the line at marriage, for both theological and practical reasons. Practically speaking, the traditions of a Mormon lifestyle and the traditions of an Evangelical lifestyle will inevitably create conflict, and this is not the kind of environment in which children should be brought up. We would say the same to a Catholic-Protestant wedding or a theist-atheist wedding, for that matter. Additionally, there are enough differences between our faiths, as we have suggested, that the attempt to blend our doctrinal differences in the intimacy required by marriage, that is, to be "unequally yoked together," would be extremely difficult and usually painful.

QUESTION: I've seen men and women respond to an evangelist's invitation to receive Christ and then walk to the front of the room or stadium. What is happening at that moment? How often can (should) such a thing take place in a person's life?

GREG: In the Evangelical tradition, it is possible for a person to have many such experiences. For example, a child might "get saved" at a summer Bible camp and have a truly emotional experience with Jesus. As they grow older, they may feel the need to express that commitment in a more mature way and respond to an invitation at their church or some other evangelistic meeting. In fact, however, Evangelicals believe that when a genuine decision for Christ is made, whether as a child or later in life, a person will only be saved once. If as a child you were saved, more than likely a later experience in life will be more of a rededication to that which you may have strayed from or that which you did not fully understand. Let me say something about the experience itself. I really appreciate your desire, as a Latter-day Saint, to better understand this important facet of the Evangelical life. Regardless of the type of meeting or experience, we believe that when the Holy Spirit calls a person to faith in Christ this is a profound and supernatural moment. I refer to this experience as "a close encounter of the divine kind."

The experience of coming to Christ or "being saved" culminates in God's greatest agenda for any human being, a time to acknowledge one's personal sin, the need for a Savior, and a willingness to surrender their life to the will and purpose of a holy God. It is often the case that there is a good deal of emotion displayed at such a time—tears are shed and a sense of heaviness is felt as one acknowledges the burden of their sin, as well as the delight and joy that come in discovering that Jesus has paid the price to take away that sin. In the words of the psalmist "Happy is the man whose sin the Lord remembers no more" (Psalms 32:1). One more thing: Sometimes I fear that many Latter-day Saints have caricatured this experience and maybe even made fun of it because it is different from their own experience of gaining a testimony. For example, I find that Mormons speak often of "becoming a member of the Church" whereas Evangelicals will speak of "coming to Jesus," and to us this is a very sacred encounter.

QUESTION: This question is for Mr. Millet. Your argument that you believe in the saving grace of Jesus Christ is convincing, and yet I have met many, many Mormons who speak a great deal about their "worthiness." Worthiness is not a concept that Evangelicals speak of very much, and yet it seems a near obsession with Mormons. I'd be interested in your response.

BOB: I've thought about this a great deal and have sought to find a parallel within Evangelicalism for the LDS concept of worthiness. An Evangelical who gives his or her heart to Christ and becomes a dedicated disciple is said to be saved. That is not a concept that would be spoken of much in LDS settings. And yet I understand completely what is intended by the idea. My search of the scriptures, both the Bible and LDS scriptures, teaches me that salvation has at least three phases or tenses—past, present, and future. The sins of my past have been forgiven through the atoning blood of Jesus and my repentance, and in that regard I have been saved from past sins. To the extent that the Holy Spirit dwells within my heart and serves, in a sense, as God's "earnest money" on me—deity's divine decree that he fully intends to purchase my soul and secure my salvation—to that extent, I am living in a saved condition in the present (see 2 Corinthians 1:21-22; 5:5; Ephesians 1:13-14). I'm pretty certain that my Evangelical friends would agree that the ultimate salvation or glorification of the Christian lies ahead, beyond the resurrection.

Now, back to our question. In a very real way, when a Latter-day Saint concerns himself or herself with worthiness, almost without realizing it they are concerning themselves with the degree to which they're living currently in a saved condition, a condition in which their covenant with Christ is intact and they are on course for the ultimate salvation and glorification hereafter. No one should misunderstand the LDS emphasis on worthiness: if we know our scriptures and the words of the prophets as we should, we are fully aware that no individual can make themselves worthy. We sing in Handel's anthem, "Worthy is the Lamb!" Worthiness comes through the proper application and incorporation of the Atonement of our Lord and Savior Jesus Christ. There's nothing wrong with saying that a man or woman is either righteous or worthy when in fact what we mean is that their life is devoted to the Lord and to building up His kingdom and establishing greater righteousness in the earth. The

Bible uses the word "worthy" often. My guess is that an Evangelical who claims to have received Christ as Savior but who has violated every major law of morality and decency, who spurns the scripture, and who refuses any and all efforts to get him to change his ways would not be considered "worthy" of the Christian designation.

Let me add that this matter is not just highbrow theology; it has very practical applications. If my trust is in me, in my achievements, in my accomplishments, then it is inevitable that I will live and die tired, run down, discouraged, and hopeless. I will always fall short. On the other hand, there is something wonderful and lifting and liberating about the promise in Romans 5:1 that through being justified by faith—being made right with God through the powers of the Atonement—we have peace with God through our Lord Jesus Christ. Peace. The kind of peace the world cannot give. The kind of peace that comes from leaning and relying upon the merits and mercy of the only Person to never take a backward step, the only person empowered and qualified to save my soul.

QUESTION: This question is for Pastor Johnson. Why do people in your faith spend so much time and effort fighting against Mormonism with book-lets, books, and videos? I don't think Mormons tend to do that very much, do they? Wouldn't people's time and energy be better spent in trying to make friends or build bridges?

GREG: I appreciate the concern expressed in your question. There are a couple of ways to look at the issue. First, there are those who seek to share with Latter-day Saints their concerns about LDS doc-trines or teachings; I want to suggest that many of these folks are sincerely concerned and feel it is im-portant to communicate those concerns in an effort to help someone become a true Christian. And while their approach may not be pleasing to members of the LDS Church, keeping in mind the concept of agency, I would hope that Mormon people would attempt to understand their motive. But let me also say that a lot of effort expended in the arena of con-frontation can be less than helpful. I am convinced that when people are in relationship they have a far greater chance of communicating with and influ-encing others, particularly in the pursuit of spiritual truth. So to the Evangelical community I would ask that we be more empathetic of the Mormons' feelings when we attempt to share with them where we think they are wrong. Remember the message of Proverbs 18:19: "A brother offended is harder to be won than a strong city; and their contentions are like the bars of a castle."

Question: If a Mormon believes that baptism is not what saves a person, why do Mormons place so much emphasis on baptizing the dead?

Bob: Latter-day Saints believe that baptism is an essential ordinance, one required for salvation. To be sure, it does not add to the Atonement, is not an extra work of some sort, but flows naturally from faith and repentance. It is a part of the faith package. Baptism is the outward symbol of my personal, inner covenant with Jesus Christ. Because we believe that baptism is essential for all men and women, because we take seriously the Savior's words to Nicodemus that one must be born of water and of the Spirit to enter the kingdom of God (John 3:5), we feel the need to make baptism available to those who have never had the opportunity in this life. This practice is inextricably linked to our belief that life and love and learning are forever, and that we continue to live in a postmortal spirit world following our death. In that world, legal administrators teach the gospel of Jesus Christ to individuals who have died, and these individuals may choose to accept or reject it. Because we believe that the ordinance of baptism is an earthly ordinance, we perform it in temples by proxy or in behalf of someone who cannot do it themselves.

QUESTION: How do our Evangelical friends interpret Amos 3:7 about God doing nothing unless He speaks through His prophets? Is the idea of a modern prophet an impossible idea for Evangelicals?

GREG: Let me suggest to you that many Evangelicals, contrary to LDS thinking, would embrace prophecy as a spiritual gift still in operation in today's church. Thus, if the gift of prophecy exists in the church, then of course there would be prophets in the church. We do not, however, have a single person in the office of prophet, as you would find in Mormonism. The verse in Amos does refer to prophets, plural. The average Evangelical would affirm both the gift of prophecy and the role of prophecy, but it would be in the capacity of a calling or a spiritual giftedness more than positional authority. In addition, we see in Luke 2 that there was a prophetess, a woman named Anna, who prophesied over the baby Jesus at the time of His blessing in the temple. This would confirm the role of prophecy as over against the position of prophet. It is also a gift that is independent of gender. From an Evangelical perspective, we do not see major prophets like Samuel or Moses or Isaiah in the New Testament, as we do in the Old Testament.

QUESTION: Greg, all denominations claim to have a valid interpretation of the Bible. How does one speak with the authority of God based on the Bible alone?

GREG: First of all, not all denominations articulate a distinctively different biblical interpretation from other Christian denominations. While I will admit that different denominations do look at some doctrinal issues with a good deal of diversity, when it comes to the fundamental teachings of Christianity, there is encouraging unity on our biblical interpretation. To be sure, a clarion dogma of the Evangelical community is the authority of the biblical text; we take biblical authority very seriously in regard to matters of faith and practice. The average Evangelical, then, would value personal Bible reading and study and feel very comfortable receiving inspiration and illumination from their time in God's word. Obviously when individual biblical interpretation challenges what has been widely understood, then it is to be assumed that the individual probably has an incorrect interpretation.

QUESTION: This question is for both of you. Matthew 5:48 says that we should be perfect as God is perfect. Do Mormons and traditional Christians have the same concept of the word perfect? How are we to accomplish what here seems to be the impossible?

BOB: I really do believe that you and I are expected to do our very best in this life, to give life our best shot. I am convinced that it is wrong to separate one's conversion to Christ from one's discipleship or to suggest that one can confess Jesus as Savior but not surrender to His commandments as Lord. Our works evidence or manifest to what extent the transforming power of Christ has worked its marvelous wonders in our lives.

The word perfect, as translated from the Greek means whole, complete, fully formed, mature. While I suppose it is hypothetically possible for a person to go through this life without making a mistake or committing a sin, it would be practically impossible; Jesus alone lived a perfect life in this sense. We become perfect "in Christ" in the sense that through joining with Him in covenant we are made whole or complete. This is why He is called the Author and Finisher of our faith. I have liabilities, while He has assets; together we have assets. I am incomplete, while He is complete; together we are complete. I am oh so imperfect, and He is completely perfect; together, Christ and I are perfect.

Greg: Obviously you can see the great influence I am having on Bob Millet, as I couldn't agree more with his answer! Interestingly, this verse has been shared with me by Latter-day Saints as an expectation that we *are* capable of human perfection in this life, but I would have to say, as Bob just did, that the perfection mentioned in Matthew 5:48 is not human perfection but rather a perfection that comes in and through Jesus Christ.

Question: Bob, you say you trust in Jesus Christ for your salvation, but your Jesus is a very different Jesus from the Jesus of your Evangelical friend. It seems to me that if you worship the wrong Jesus you go to the wrong place hereafter.

Bob: This is a fascinating question, but unfortunately one that is misleading. It's what Greg and I have come to call a conversation stopper, inasmuch as it puts the responder immediately on the defensive. But I'll try to exercise some restraint and give my best answer.

When the man on the street hears that Latterday Saints "worship a different Jesus," does he think that Mormons believe their Jesus was born in India or Russia or Cleveland or Paramus, New Jersey? Does he think that our Jesus performed no miracles, taught no great truths, performed no atonement, and is still in the grave? Just a moment's reflection and a little bit of study into LDS doctrine will reveal that Latter-day Saints clearly believe in the same historical Jesus as Catholics and Protestants do: born of the virgin Mary in Bethlehem of Judea; delivered timeless teachings and served as a matchless example of the righteous life; suffered, bled, and died for the sins of the world; rose from the dead on that first Easter morning; and will return to reign in glory as King of kings and Lord of lords. It's the same person!

Now, we do have differences between us concerning the relationship of the members within the Godhead, as we have discussed before. Our concept of how Jesus is indeed the Eternal God would be different than that of traditional Christianity, but I assure you that there is no virtue, no quality, no attribute, no divine power that your Jesus possesses that ours does not. In other words, from my perspective, they are one and the same.

QUESTION: Pastor Johnson, you mention that you are a former Latter-day Saint. What is your real motivation for meeting with Bob in this setting? Is it your hope to prove Bob and the LDS Church wrong?

GREG: Great question, but to be honest, it hurts a little bit. It hurts because the very effort Bob and I are engaged in represents a new paradigm of interaction between Evangelicals and Latter-day Saints. As such, I think we both face criticisms from our own constituencies as well as each other's. And that criticism is very often directed toward our motive and some hidden agenda. While I see where you're coming from, I point out that I have taken a great deal of flack for pursuing this kind of public interaction with Robert L. Millet. Would you like to know my agenda, my heart as a former Latter-day Saint? My heart is to build a new kind of relationship between our two faith traditions where we can really communicate with one another and yes, even influence one another. Let's be clear: I would like all Mormons to discover what I have found in my Evangelical faith, but shy of that, I want every Mormon to know that I really do love them; that I am not just looking for another notch on my spiritual belt; and that I hope that they might experience the personal, intimate relationship with Jesus Christ that I have come to know.

QUESTION: Webster's dictionary says that a Christian is one who claims Jesus Christ as their Savior. God judges the heart. Does it matter if the person wears garments or a cross on their neck if their heart is truly for Christ? What do you think, Greg?

GREG: I think you're absolutely right: God does judge the heart. The Bible teaches that man looks on the outward appearance but that God looks upon the heart (1 Samuel 16:7). So in one sense I agree: it doesn't matter whether one wears a garment or a cross. But that those symbols are significant to us does mean something to all of us. If a person were to wear a cross and suppose that the cross was saving them, they would be mistaken. Likewise, if someone who wore LDS garments thought that the garments were saving them, they would be mistaken. Let me make this comment: while I find no biblical teaching or instruction that Christians are to wear a particular garment, I likewise find no instruction to wear a cross either. I truly believe that salvation is first and foremost about a relationship with Jesus Christ; we will not take a theology quiz when we die in order to get into heaven. Nor will our good works be weighed against our sins. When we get to heaven, I believe, the questions we may all have to answer are: "What did you do with my Son? Did you know my Son? Did you take Jesus as your Savior?" In my relationship with Bob Millet, we talk less about the symbols of our faith and more about the essential teachings of Christianity.

QUESTION: This is for Professor Millet. After the crucifixion, the physical body of Jesus rose from his tomb. This did not happen with Joseph Smith. Doesn't this fact cast doubt on the LDS's Church's claim of divinity for Smith?

BOB: This won't take long. Jesus is the Christ, the Son of God, the Savior and Redeemer of all the world. We worship Him, just as we worship the Father. While Latter-day Saints believe in the divine call of Joseph Smith, we certainly do not believe that Joseph Smith was divine, nor do we in any way equate him with our Lord and Savior. We worship

God, we revere our prophets, but we do not worship them.

QUESTION: This question is for Greg. Which is more important in defining Christianity—*sola scriptura* or the historical creeds? If a doctrine can be supported by the Bible, but is not found in the creeds, is it Christian? Conversely, if a doctrine is found in the creeds but is not supported by the Bible, is it Christian?

GREG: For most Evangelicals the quick answer is: *Sola scriptura* trumps historical creeds every time. If there is a doctrinal matter in a creed that is not supported by the Bible, Evangelicals would reject the creed. At the same time, most Evangelicals, widely speaking, would believe that the statements of the best-known creeds of Christianity are completely undergirded by biblical texts and principles.

QUESTION: Bob, is it true that the current Book of Mormon has undergone changes since its original version? Why would it be necessary to revise a document given to Joseph Smith from God in which the original version was in English?

BOB: Yes, there have been many changes made in the text of the Book of Mormon since its original printing. Most all of these have to do with spelling, punctuation, or other grammatical concerns. Having studied over every change made in the Book of Mormon, I can assure you that nothing of substance in terms of doctrine has been altered. As to why alterations would be needed, the same thing has taken place with English editions of the Bible for 400 years. There have literally been hundreds of changes made in the King James Bible since 1611, and newer versions of the Bible (including paraphrases) pop up all the time.

QUESTION: Greg, when you say our LDS beliefs are "unbiblical," do you understand that this is offensive to Mormons? We study and love the Bible. Because we believe in additional books of scripture does not mean that we put down the Bible, neglect the Bible, or do not take the Bible seriously. Could you comment on this?

GREG: Certainly I understand the offense a Latter-day Saint feels when their teachings are labeled as unbiblical. The Evangelical Christian is not simply troubled by additional books of scripture alongside the Bible, but I really do believe that we see various teachings of the LDS Church as unbiblical. For example, the way you view the nature of the Godhead, the refusal to accept *creatio ex nihilo*, the "fortunate fall" of Adam and Eve, and the widely held view of a works righteousness—these would be considered unbiblical to us. If we Evangelicals and Latter-day Saints are serious about understanding one another and sincere in our desire to influence one another, we both must do the hard work of suspending our emotional reaction to what we disagree over and be willing to wrestle through the differences without reacting emotionally.

QUESTION: If revelation continued after Christ, how are the verses in Revelation 22:18-19 that speak about adding to or taking away from the scripture understood by Mormons?

BOB: Similar restrictions regarding adding to or taking away from scripture are to found in Deuteronomy 4:2 and 12:32. If those verses were to be taken at face value, then 61 books in the Old and New Testaments should be jettisoned. Clearly Moses is talking about adding to the law of God, or in this case the Pentateuch. Similarly, any good New Testament commentary will clarify that the prohibition in Revelation 22 refers not at all to the Bible but to "the words of the prophecy of this book," meaning the Apocalypse or Revelation of John.

QUESTION: Maybe this is a tough question, but what do you each feel is the most important thing you have learned from the other?

GREG: To quote our friend, Dr. Richard Mouw from Fuller Seminary, my relationship with Robert Millet has been "one of God's little surprises." I could never have imagined on 14 April 1997, when I met Bob for the first time at BYU, that the kind of friendship and relationship that has emerged between us would even be possible. We've traveled many miles together, shared many experiences together, and we've given each other the gifts of honest inquiry and vulnerable reflection about the most important matter in each of our lives. To experience the gift of friendship with someone you disagree with or with whom you have honest theological differences has been for me one of life's most enriching and broadening endeavors. I truly believe I am a better person, a more caring person, and, yes, even more theologically acute because of Bob Millet; for that I very grateful to him.

BOB: There is so much I could say here, but I'll use some discipline and be brief. Greg has taught me what it means to do what is right and let the consequence follow, to seek the will of God and then carry it out, no matter the obstacles. He has con-firmed in my mind and heart just how vital it is to have Jesus Christ as the Divine Center of our lives. He has helped me, more than any other mortal, to understand and experience how to hold tenaciously to one's faith and yet allow the Spirit of Christ to broaden our vistas and expand our horizons.

QUESTION: As things become increasingly turbu-lent in our society and Judeo-Christian standards and beliefs are progressively attacked, do you see the LDS and Evangelical traditions (and, hopefully, others) putting aside theological differences and forming closer ties in order to stand boldly against such rising tides?

BOB: All I can say is that I genuinely hope so. There is so much that our two faith traditions agree on in terms of marriage and family and morality and absolute truths, that it would be a great tragedy if we did not grow up and learn to work together more effectively in opposing the eroding moral values and the shifting sands of secularity.

COMMENT: I don't really have a question. I just want to say that this whole thing is refreshing to me. I have been an Evangelical Christian with a past of fifteen years (childhood) of Mormonism. I have always believed what you both are talking and preaching about. I am so excited to see this coming out in the light. We must all learn somehow to love and accept each other, even though we have our differences.

COMMENT/QUESTION: I'd like to thank you both for what has taken place here tonight. I think this is what Jesus would have us do. My heart has been touched with a desire to build better relationships with my Mormon friends. We get along okay; that is, we don't fight and quarrel. But we really have not dared to open up our hearts to one another. In addition to all you have said tonight, what final suggestions would you offer?

BOB: It seems to me that a person must have a heart for this work. That is, we can go through the motions, say the right things, meet all the right people, learn all the necessary facts, and become very busy in the business of outreach, but still not further this work. Why? Because we are doing it out of a sense of responsibility or duty or assignment. I don't mean to oversimplify, but let me wax personal for a second and indicate to you that I have prayed a great deal about outreach. I have pleaded with God to forgive my sins; to cleanse my heart of prejudice and littleness of soul and double-mindedness and ego and arrogance; to rid my mind of all predetermined agendas and ulterior motives; to give me the bigger picture; and, most important, to endow me with a portion of the pure love of Christ. I have asked God specifically to see persons of other faiths as He sees them and to love them as He loves them. To some extent my prayers have been answered. I love this work. I enjoy it. I find it both stimulating and deeply rewarding. I must be honest and confess that a part of me is frightened by outreach, for my inadequacy and my ignorance are ever before me; I fear that I will misrepresent the Church or embarrass the university, or stumble and thereby reflect poorly upon both. On the other hand, I have felt a sustaining influence, a divine enabling power that has quickened my mind and expanded my heart. While some may disagree with me, I believe strongly that the Spirit of Christ has brooded over this work.

GREG: Let me begin by suggesting that your efforts in this area must be intentional. By that I mean, in your work environment, in your community, in your family there are people you must desire to engage in theological discussions. Obviously this is a relational enterprise; you can't do this with a hundred people or fifty people, but you can with several people, and especially with one. Just think of the enormous good that could be accomplished and the level of understanding that could be increased. That's my hope, and I'm quite certain it's Bob's hope as well.

Here's a fascinating thought. It is said that there are approximately 700 million Evangelicals in the world and about 13 million Mormons. If we could just get 13 million Evangelicals to develop a deep friendship with one Latter-day Saint, every Latter-day Saint in the world would have at least one Evangelical friend.

PART IV
Conclusion

I N THE LATE 1970s, Professor Truman Madsen, the first holder of the Richard L. Evans Chair of Religious Understanding, organized a conference at BYU on Mormonism. Participants included such non-LDS scholars as Robert Bellah, Abraham Kaplan, Jacob Milgrom, David Noel Freedman, W. D. Davies, James Charlesworth, and Krister Stendahl. Stendahl was then serving as Dean of the Harvard Divinity School. Over the years that followed, Truman maintained contact and developed friendships with many of the presenters.

Some years after his departure from the divinity school, Stendahl was appointed as Bishop of Sweden. During that same time period The Church of Jesus Christ of Latter-day Saints announced that a temple would be built in Stockholm, and, as is often the case, there was a good deal of reaction from the public, much of it negative. Bishop Stendahl convened a press conference in one of the LDS chapels. He called upon his people to be more open, more respectful, less critical of the Latter-day Saints, and to ponder upon the implications of a religious group whose care and concern for the spiritual welfare of humankind spanned the veil of death. In regard to the hostile press that the LDS Church had been receiving, he offered three simple but thoughtful bits of advice:

1. If you want to know something about another person's faith or beliefs, ask an active, participating, and somewhat knowledgeable member of that faith.

2. If you intend to compare the merits of one faith with another, be sure to compare your best with their best.

3. Always leave room for "holy envy."

Now to be sure, there is a risk associated with learning something new about someone else. New insights always affect old perspectives, and thus some rethinking, rearranging, and restructuring of our worldviews are inevitable. When we look beyond a man or woman's color or ethnic group or social circle or church or creed or statement of belief, when we try our best to see them for who and what they are, children of the same God, something good and worthwhile happens within us, and we are thereby drawn into a closer union with the God of us all. In short, such a risk is extremely rewarding.

Both of us feel a sense of responsibility now that we didn't feel five years ago. Being a religion professor, Bob mentioned that it is not unusual at a university as large as BYU, with some 30,000 students, to have young people make comments several times during the semester about other churches, and some of those comments be inappropriate and/or inaccurate. "Well, you know how the Baptists are, they believe that once you are saved it doesn't matter how you live." Bob felt a sense of responsibility, if that person had indeed voiced the Baptist views incorrectly, to say, "Can we talk about that for just a minute? You know, they don't really believe that. They believe this and this and this." And then he said: "And I don't mean for this to hurt your feelings personally, but we don't want to be misrepresented. Why would we want to misrepresent them?" Our Evangelical friends feel the same sense of responsibility if they are in conversation and someone says, "You know the Mormons, they believe . . . ." We would hope the instructor would say, "I'm not sure that's what they believe at all. In fact, I'm pretty certain it's not what they believe, because I happen to know a Latter-day Saint, and that's not at all where he's coming from." Now that doesn't sound like much, but that's a pretty good start in terms of trying to straighten out much of the misperception that underlies misunderstanding. In short, what this entire process has added to us is a burden of responsibility to love our neighbor enough to be sure that those over whom we have responsibility, namely our students or our colleagues, better understand the beliefs held sacred by those of other faiths. When we love people, we begin to feel a Christian responsibility for them—for their welfare, for their safety, and even for their reputation and good name.

As a reader, you need to understand that we have never been more committed to our own faith traditions than we are right now, today. At the same time, we have never been more liberal-minded than we are right now, in the proper sense of that word liberal—we have never been more convinced that God is working through good men and women all over the earth to accomplish His purposes and build up His kingdom. We know there is a God and that salvation comes in and through the atoning blood of Christ, and in no other way. But we also know, as C.S. Lewis once stated, that there are many people even outside the ranks of Christianity who are being led by God's "secret influence" to focus on those aspects of their religion that are in agreement with Christianity and, as he said, "who thus belong to Christ without knowing it."

Now that requires a stretching of our typical worldview, a broadening of our horizons and a loosening of our categories. But in fact, the older we get, the less prone we are to believe in coincidence. Like you, we believe that the Almighty has a divine plan, not only for the ultimate establishment of the kingdom of God on earth, but also an individualized plan for you and me. We gladly and eagerly acknowledge His hand in all things, including the orchestration of events in our lives and the interlacing of our daily associations. We believe He brings people into our path who can bless and enlighten us, and we know He brings us into contact with people whose acquaintanceship will, down the road, open doors, dissolve barriers, and make strait the way of the Lord. The prayer of Elisha for his young companion seems particularly pertinent to this kind of work: "Lord, I pray thee, open [our] eyes that [we] may see" (2 Kings 6:17).

DOCTRINAL PARAMETERS
WITHIN MORMONISM

Robert L. Millet

THE CENTRAL, SAVING doctrine is that Jesus is the Christ, the Son of God, the Savior and Redeemer of humankind; that He lived, taught, healed, suffered and died for our sins; and that He rose from the dead the third day with an immortal, resurrected body (1 Corinthians 15:1-3; D&C 76:40-42). It was Joseph Smith who spoke of these central truths as the "fundamental principles" of our religion to which all other doctrines are but appendages (*Teachings of the Prophet Joseph Smith*, Deseret Book, 1976, 121). There is power in doctrine, power in the word, power to heal the wounded soul, power to transform human behavior.

"True doctrine, understood, changes attitudes and behavior," Elder Boyd K. Packer explained. "The study of the doctrines of the gospel will improve behavior quicker than a study of behavior will improve behavior. That is why we stress so forcefully the study of the doctrines of the gospel" (*Conference Report*, October 1986, 20). Elder Neal A. Maxwell also pointed out that "Doctrines believed and practiced do change and improve us, while insuring our vital access to the Spirit. Both outcomes are crucial" (*One More Strain of Praise*, Bookcraft, 1999, x).

Doctrinal Parameters

L ATTER-DAY SAINTS ARE not in the line of historic Christianity and thus are neither Catholic nor Protestant. We believe in scripture beyond the Bible and in continuing revelation through apostles and prophets. We do not accept the concepts concerning God, Christ, and the Godhead that grew out of the post-New Testament church councils. All of these things constitute reasons why many Protestants and Catholics label us as non-Christian. There is another reason we are suspect, one that underlies and buttresses large amounts of anti-Mormon propaganda, namely, what they perceive to be some of our "unusual doctrines," many of which were presented by a few Church leaders of the past.

In determining what Latter-day Saints believe to be the doctrine of their Church, consider: Is it found within the four standard works? Within official declarations or proclamations? Is it taught or discussed in general conference or other official gatherings by general Church leaders today? Is it found in the general handbooks or approved curriculum of the Church today? If it meets at least one of these criteria, we can feel secure and appropriate about teaching it.

Loyalty to Imperfect Leaders

ORMONS BELIEVE WE can sustain with
all our hearts the prophets and apostles
without believing that they are perfect
or that everything they say or do is exactly what God
wants said and done. In short, we do not believe in
apostolic or prophetic infallibility. "I can fellowship
the President of the Church," said Lorenzo Snow, "if
he does not know everything I know. . . . I saw the
. . . imperfections in [Joseph Smith]. . . . I thanked
God that he would put upon a man who had those
imperfections the power and authority he placed
upon him . . . for I knew that I myself had weakness,
and I thought there was a chance for me" (cited by
Maxwell, *Conference Report*, October 1984, 10).

Every member of the Church, including those
called to guide its destiny, has the right to be wrong
at one time or another—to say something that simply isn't true. They also have the right to improve
their views, to change their minds and correct mistakes, to refine and clarify matters as new light and
new truth become available. Joseph Smith once remarked: "I did not like the old man [a brother Pela-
tiah Brown] being called up for erring in doctrine.

. . . It does not prove that a man is not a good man because he errs in doctrine" (*History of the Church* 5:340). Being called as an apostle or even as President of the Church does not remove the man from mortality or make him perfect. President David O. McKay explained that "when God makes the prophet He does not unmake the man" (*Conference Report*, April 1907, 11-12; October 1912, 121; April 1962, 7). "With all their inspiration and greatness," Bruce R. McConkie declared, "prophets are yet mortal men with imperfections common to mankind in general. They have their opinions and prejudices and are left to work out their problems without inspiration in many instances" (*Mormon Doctrine*, 2nd ed., 1966, 608).

President Gordon B. Hinckley stated: "I have worked with seven Presidents of this Church. I have recognized that all have been human. But I have never been concerned over this. They may have had some weaknesses. But this has never troubled me. I know that the God of heaven has used mortal men throughout history to accomplish His divine purposes" (*Conference Report*, April 1992, 77). On another occasion President Hinckley pleaded with the Saints that "as we continue our search for truth . . . we look for strength and goodness rather than weakness and foibles in those who did so great a work in their time. We recognize that our forebears were human. They doubtless made mistakes. . . . There was only one perfect man who ever walked the earth. The Lord has used imperfect people in the process of building his perfect society. If some of them occasionally stumbled, or if their characters may have been slightly flawed in one way or another, the wonder is the greater that they accomplished so much" ("The Continuous Pursuit of Truth," *Ensign*, April 1986, 5).

Some years ago my colleague Joseph McConkie remarked to a group of religious educators: "We have the scholarship of the early brethren to build upon; we have the advantage of additional history; we have inched our way up the mountain of our destiny and now stand in a position to see things with greater clarity than did they. . . . We live in finer houses than did our pioneer forefathers, but this does not argue that we are better or that our rewards will be greater. In like manner our understanding of gospel principles should be better housed, and we should constantly be seeking to make it so. There is no honor in our reading by oil lamps when we have been granted better light." ("The Gathering of Israel and the Second Coming of Christ," Church Educational

System Address, August 1982, Typescript, 3, 5). Thus it is important to note that ultimately the Lord will hold us responsible for the teachings and direction and focus provided by the living oracles of our own day, both in terms of their commentary upon canonized scripture, as well as the living scripture that is delivered through them by the power of the Holy Ghost (D&C 68:3-4).

Facing Hard Issues

Most Latter-day Saints are eager to sustain and uphold their leaders. Consequently, we are especially hesitant to suggest that something taught by Brigham Young or Orson Pratt or Orson Hyde might not be in harmony with the truth as God has made it known to us "line upon line, precept upon precept" (Isaiah 28:10; 2 Nephi 28:30). Some time ago a colleague and I were in southern California speaking to a group of about 500 people, both Latter-day Saint and Protestant. During the question and answer phase of the program, someone asked the inevitable: "Are you really Christian? Do you, as many claim, worship a different Jesus?" I explained that we worship the Christ of the New Testament, that we believe wholeheartedly in His virgin birth, His divine Sonship, His miracles, His transforming teachings, His atoning sacrifice, and His bodily resurrection from the dead. I added that we also believe in the teachings of and about Christ found in the Book of Mormon and modern revelation. After the meeting an LDS woman came up to me and said: "You didn't tell the truth about what we believe!" Startled, I asked: "What do you mean?" She responded: "You said we believe in the virgin birth of Christ, and you know very well that we don't believe that." "Yes we do," I retorted. She then said with a great deal of emotion: "I want to believe you, but people have told me for years that we believe that God the Father had sexual relations with Mary and thereby Jesus was conceived." I looked her in the eyes and said: "I'm aware of that teaching, but that is not the doctrine of the Church; that is not what we teach in the Church today. Have you ever heard the Brethren teach it in conference? Is it in the standard works, the curricular materials, or the handbooks of the Church? Is it a part of an official declaration or proclamation?" I watched what seemed like a 500-pound weight come off her shoulders, as tears came into her eyes, and she simply said: "Thank you, Brother Millet."

I have no hesitation telling an individual or a group "I don't know" when I am asked why men are ordained to the priesthood and women are not; why Blacks were denied the blessings of the priesthood for almost a century and a half; and several other matters that have neither been revealed nor clarified by those holding the proper keys. The difficulty comes when someone in the past *has* spoken on these matters, *has* put forward ideas that are out of harmony with what we know and teach today, and when those teachings are still available, either in print or among the everyday conversations of the members, and have never been corrected or clarified.

It's inevitable that some persons, either Latter-day Saints or those of other faiths, who are told that not everything stated by an LDS prophet or apostle is a part of the doctrine of the Church and of what we teach today, will be troubled and ask follow-up questions: "Well then, what *else* did this Church leader teach that is not considered doctrine today? How can we confidently accept anything else he taught? What other directions taken or procedures pursued by the Church in an earlier time do we not follow in our day?" The fact is, one need not take such an approach. This is like throwing the baby out with the bath water. We must never allow ourselves to over-generalize and thus overreact. Nor must we be guilty of discounting all that is good and uplifting and divinely given because of an aberration. After all, because a prophet once expressed an opinion or perhaps even put forward a doctrinal view that needed further clarification or even correction, does not invalidate all else that he did or said. I would certainly hate to be judged that way and have no desire to be guilty of doing the same to the Lord's anointed. God calls His prophets, and God corrects them. He knows their strengths, and He knows their weakness.

Those of other faiths who leap to criticize the Church and question its truthfulness because of past teachings from Church leaders that are not accepted as doctrine today, would do well to ask themselves if they are prepared to apply the same standards of judgment to their own tradition, their own prominent speakers, or their own past. This is like asking someone, "Would you like to better understand Roman Catholicism today? Then study carefully the atrocities of the Crusades or the horrors of the Inquisition." Or: "Would you like a deeper glimpse into the hearts of Lutherans today? Then make it your business to study the anti-Semitic writings of Martin Luther." Or: "Would you care to better understand where Southern Baptists are coming from? Then simply read the many sermons of Baptist preachers during the time of the Civil War who utilized biblical passages to justify the practice of slavery."

True doctrine has what might be called "sticking power"—it is taught and discussed and perpetuated over time, and with the passing of years seems to take on greater significance. Time, experience, careful and ponderous thought, and subsequent revelation through prophets—these all either reinforce and support, or bring into question and eventually discount a particular idea. For example, doctrines such as the proper relationship between the grace of God and the good works of man, the redemption of the dead, exaltation through eternal marriage, and the overall significance of temples—these matters have been discussed and clarified and reinforced by those holding the keys of the kingdom, to such extent that we not only accept them fully as true and from God, but we also grasp their profundity even more than when they were first made known. Falsehood and error will eventually be detected and dismissed by those charged to guide the destiny of the kingdom of God, but truth, as Joseph Smith observed, "will cut its own way" (*Teachings of the Prophet Joseph Smith*, 313).

OTHER ILLUSTRATIONS

I WAS RAISED in the Church and was well aware of the priesthood restriction for black members of the Church. For as long as I can remember, the explanation for why our black brothers and sisters were denied the full blessings of the priesthood (including the temple) was some variation of the theme that they had been less valiant in the premortal life and thus had come to earth under a curse, an explanation that has been perpetuated as doctrine for most of our Church's history. In June of 1978 everything changed—not just the matter of who could or could not be ordained to the priesthood, but also the nature of the explanation for why the restriction had been in place from the beginning. Elder Dallin H. Oaks, in a 1988 interview, was asked: "As much as any doctrine the Church has espoused, or controversy the Church has been embroiled in, this one [the priesthood restriction] seems to stand out. Church members seemed to have less to go on to get a grasp of the issue. Can you address why this was the case, and what can be learned from it?" In response, Elder Oaks stated that "If you read the scriptures with this question in mind, 'Why did the Lord command this or why did he command that,' you find that in less than one in a hundred commands was any reason given. It's not the pattern of the Lord to give reasons. We can put reasons to revelation. We can put reasons to commandments. When we do we're on our own. Some people put reasons to the one we're talking about here, and they turned out to be spectacularly wrong. There is a lesson in that. The lesson I've drawn . . . [is that] I decided a long time ago that I had faith in the command and I had no faith in the reasons that had been suggested for it."

Then came a follow-up question: "Are you referring to reasons given even by general authorities?" Elder Oaks answered: "Sure. I'm referring to reasons given by general authorities and reasons elaborated upon that reason by others. The whole set of reasons seemed to me to be unnecessary risk-taking. . . . Let's don't make the mistake that's been made in the past, here and in other areas, trying to put reasons to revelation. The reasons turn out to be man-made to a great extent. The revelations are what we sustain as the will of the Lord and that's where safety lies" (*Provo Daily Herald*, 5 June 1988, 21).

In other words, we really do not know why the restriction on the priesthood existed. The First Presidency stated in January 1970 that the priesthood was restricted "for reasons which we believe are known to God, but which he has not made fully known to man." I have come to realize that this is what Elder McConkie meant in his August 1978 address to the Church Educational System when he counseled us to "Forget everything that I have said, or what President Brigham Young or President George Q. Cannon or whosoever has said in days past that is contrary to the present revelation. We spoke with a limited understanding and without the light and knowledge that now has come into the world.

"We get our truth and our light line upon line and precept upon precept. We have now had added a new flood of intelligence and light on this particular subject, and it erases all the darkness and all the views and all the thoughts of the past. They don't matter any more. . . . It is a new day and a new arrangement, and the Lord has now given the revelation that sheds light out into the world on this subject. As to any slivers of light or any particles of darkness of the past, we forget about them" (Cited in *Priesthood*, Deseret Book, 1981, 132).

Let's take another question: Was Jesus married? The scriptures do not provide an answer. "We do not know anything about Jesus Christ being married," President Charles W. Penrose stated in 1912. "The Church has no authoritative declaration on the subject" (*Improvement Era*, September 1912, 1042). More recently, at the time that the book and movie, *The DaVinci Code*, were stirring up feelings all across the globe, the First Presidency of the LDS Church issued a statement that said, in essence: The scriptures are silent as to whether Jesus Christ was married. It is true that some early Church leaders gave their opinion on the matter, but those opinions did not then, nor do they now, represent the doctrine of the Church. So whether Jesus was or was not married is not part of the doctrine of the Church. It would be well for us to apply the following lesson from President Harold B. Lee: "With respect to doctrines and meanings of scriptures, let me give you a safe counsel. It is usually not well to use a single passage of scripture [or, I would add, isolated sermons] in proof of a point of doctrine unless it is confirmed by modern revelation or by the Book of Mormon. . . . To single out a passage of scripture to prove a point, unless it is [so] confirmed . . . is always a hazardous thing" (*Teachings of Harold B. Lee*, Bookcraft, 1996, 157).

Conclusion

I STATE TO my classes regularly that it is as important for us to know *what we do not know* as it is for us to know what we know. Far too many things are taught or discussed or even argued about that fit into the realm of the unrevealed and thus the unresolved. Such matters, particularly if they do not fall within that range of revealed truth we teach today, do not edify or inspire. Often, very often, they lead to confusion and sow discord. This does not, however, in any way suggest that we should not seek to study and grow and expand in our gospel understanding, to gain what Peter called a *reason* for the *hope* within us (1 Peter 3:15), a personal witness that is as settling to the mind as it is soothing to the heart. In that spirit, Hugh B. Brown once wrote: "I am impressed with the testimony of a man who can stand and say he knows the gospel is true. But what I would like to ask is 'But, sir, do you know the gospel?' . . . Mere testimony can be gained with but perfunctory knowledge of the Church and its teachings. . . . But to retain a testimony, to be of service in building the Lord's kingdom, requires a serious study of the gospel and knowing what it is" (Personal Correspondence to Robert J. Matthews, 28 January 1969).

There is a valid reason why it is difficult to "tie down" Latter-day Saint doctrine, one that derives from the very nature of the Restoration. The fact that God continues to speak through his anointed servants; the fact that He, through those servants, continues to reveal, elucidate, and clarify what has already been given; and the fact that our canon of scripture is open, flexible, and expanding—all of this militates against what many in the Christian world would call a systematic theology. The teaching and application of sound doctrine are great safeguards to us in these last days, shields against the fiery darts of the adversary. Understanding true doctrine and being true to that doctrine can keep us from ignorance, from error, and from sin. The Apostle Paul counseled Timothy: "If thou put the brethren [and sisters] in remembrance of these things, thou shalt be a good minister of Jesus Christ, nourished up in the word of faith and of good doctrine whereunto thou hast attained. . . . Till I come, give attendance to reading, to exhortation, to doctrine." (1 Timothy 4:6, 13.)

IMAGINE WHAT GOD COULD DO!

Gregory C.V. Johnson

OVER THE YEARS I have felt the discouragement that many pastors in Utah feel, namely, that our efforts are having very little spiritual impact on the larger culture. Clearly, there are those brief moments of victory, but they were occasional, periodic, and could hardly be described as dramatic or revivalistic. The task for the Evangelical church here is to reach Mormon people, Latter-day Saints, with the gospel, to help them understand orthodox Christianity and its differences with The Church of Jesus Christ of Latter-day Saints. I remember hearing from a Utah Christian leader during the Fall of 2000 that at best Protestant Christianity was roughly 2% of the population of Utah at the beginning of the 1900s, and as I calculated by rough estimations the presence of Evangelical Christianity in Utah 100 years later, I realized that our presence remained no greater than 2% of the population. In other words, in a state with a population of 2.5 million people, around 60% of the population are Mormons and 20,000 are Evangelical.

No matter how I looked at our situation in Utah, again and again I felt something was wrong, something needed to change, God and His church could surely do better, and that it was time for the Evangelical church of Utah to take a long hard look at itself in the proverbial mirror and ask itself some pretty tough questions. Since the fall of 2000, I've been on a quest, and I sense like never before that God is hearing and answering the prayers of His church in Utah. There is a growing sense among many Evangelical pastors and churches that indeed it is time to change our methods, change our strategy, change our perspective, humble ourselves before each other and our culture, and leave God to do what He alone is capable of doing. We need to set aside our own agendas and attitudes in order that the agenda and heart of Jesus Christ might prevail in this amazingly beautiful place called Utah.

While I write as an Evangelical, wholly committed to my faith tradition and understanding of orthodox, historical biblical Christianity, I want to write in a way that encourages and inspires both an Evangelical and a Latter-day Saint audience. I have come to learn in my ministry here in Utah that the issue is not only that there are theological differences between Mormons and Evangelicals, but, equally important, how we engage those differences. Recently, in a conversation with a Latter-day Saint (LDS) general authority by the name of Elder Robert Wood, he expressed the same sentiment. He said it was not that Evangelicals attempt to share their faith with members of his church that bothered him; in fact, he said he would be offended if a person believed he had the truth and avoided sharing it with others. Rather, the issue is *how* others attempt to share their doctrinal concerns with Mormon people that often causes conflict. As a former Mormon myself, who came to embrace an Evangelical perspective in my teens, I concur with Elder Wood: it is far more often our approach that causes hurt and tensions than the fact that we do have differing views. So, it is my hope that Evangelicals and Mormons alike might read what follows with equal appreciation for the challenges we have in conversing with each other in a fair and respectful way.

Additionally, I would like to hold out the hope that God is bigger than our own individual perspectives and might very well do something amongst us that we never expected or find hard to imagine. Indeed, to my Mormon friends and my own Evangelical community, just imagine what God could do if we would just let Him! Is it possible that the Lord of the universe might work a miracle that would allow us to reach out to each other, not as enemies to be conquered, but rather as brothers and sisters in common love of Jesus Christ? Yes, I hear you: I know we are not there yet. Yes, I know there are important doctrinal matters for us to discuss and clarify. Yes, I realize we may never achieve complete doctrinal harmony. I do believe, however, in a big God and would like to believe that in a world that grows increasingly hostile against traditional values and morals, we Evangelicals and our LDS friends could achieve significant things together if we were more united in biblical truth. Without question, the shared values and morals that both Evangelicals and Latter-day Saints hold dear are under sustained attack from a hostile, unregenerate world, and if we do not discover ways to come together, we will surely suffer together.

A Glimpse at the Past

To get right to the point, Evangelicals and Mormons have had a conflicted past. The very beginnings of Mormonism set the stage for Evangelical Protestants to reject the teachings of Joseph Smith. According to Smith, as a boy of 14, he inquired of the Lord as to what church he should affiliate himself with. In a vision he was told to join none of them, as they were all wrong and that their creeds were an abomination to God (see *Pearl of Great Price*, Joseph Smith-History 1:19). Joseph continued to affirm this vision, and declare that God had chosen him as a modern prophet to restore the fullness of Christianity to the earth between 1820 and 1830. He eventually organized what he believed to be the true church of Jesus Christ in April of 1830. It is no wonder that Protestant Christianity was offended and dismissive of the claims of Joseph Smith. As the teachings of Mormonism became more clearly defined as distinct from biblical orthodoxy—in particular the doctrine of God's nature, an emphasis on works as essential to salvation, and the practice of plural marriage, to name a few—Protestants rejected Smith and his teachings as heretical and cultic. Thus, Mormons were targeted as enemies of the faith and driven from one locale to the next, eventually arriving in the Salt Lake Valley under the leadership of the faith's second leader, Brigham Young, after the murder of Joseph Smith in Carthage, Illinois.

As the nation expanded west and Utah sought statehood, Mormonism once again encountered the disdain of other Christian communities because of their doctrines and practices. Even after formally abandoning the practice of polygamy in 1890, Protestants maintained their strong disdain for Mormonism and the faith of Joseph Smith. While animosity between Evangelicals and Mormons has been the name of the game throughout the existence of Mormonism, it could be said that hostilities and tensions between the two faith communities found new life during the latter part of the 20th century, particularly under the leadership and ministry of Walter Martin, the famed "Bible Answer Man," and also through the spread of the anti-Mormon video, "The Godmakers."

From the late 60's to the late 80's Walter Martin and the ministry he led, Christian Research Institute (CRI), gave new life to tensions between Evangelicalism and Mormonism. Walter Martin became the man every Mormon loved to hate, as he denounced and regularly challenged Latter-day Saints and their doctrines as non-Christian during his radio broadcasts. Martin often said that the Protestant community had been soundly asleep as the "cults" (traditionally meant to refer to such groups as Mormonism, Jehovah Witnesses, Christian Scientists, etc.) prospered and gained converts from traditional Christianity. As his influence grew, Martin literally sounded the battle cry, and various ministries to reach the "cults" began during this time with Martin as their champion and leader. Having left Mormonism in early 1981 as a 14-year-old boy myself, I became quite involved in this movement and was deeply moved by its passion and urgency to reach those who had been misled by unorthodox expressions of Christianity. I became a youthful zealot in my attempts to reach Mormons with true Christianity. I was privileged to meet Martin personally on several occasions during this period and regularly witnessed to Mormons with confrontational methods of apologetics and evangelism.

Mormons began to defend themselves against this renewed hostility by producing such books as *Mormons Are Christians Too*, *Mormons are Christians Because*, and, perhaps most famously, Stephen Robinson's book, *Are Mormons Christians?* These books and other efforts by Mormon apologists suggested that Mormonism had every right to call itself Christian and that such efforts to attack Mormonism were simply an affirmation of Mormonism's truthfulness. Mormons simply dismissed the charges that they were not Christians as modern day expressions of anti-Mormonism. Offended Protestants had attacked the Mormon community in its early history, and, believing that Mormonism represented true restored latter-day Christianity, it was being assaulted once again.

There is a phenomenon that is often referred to by Evangelical pastors and churches in Utah known as "kicking over the beehive." What is meant by this phrase is that a growing number of Utah-based Evangelical churches and ministries began to tire of having outside mission groups come to Utah to stir up tensions, engage polemically, and then depart to their points of origin triumphantly. It could be said that Evangelical churches in Utah during the early 1990's began to separate themselves in growing numbers from the counter-cult movements because it became increasingly difficult to engage the culture of Utah while such feelings of animosity prevailed.

Having graduated from Denver Theological Seminary in 1992, I first came to Utah as an associate pastor at Washington Heights Baptist Church, clearly one of the most successful and strategic Evangelical churches in Utah. I was honored and privileged to join the pastoral staff as the Minister of Outreach and Discipleship and was tasked with the assignment of reaching out to the Mormon community in our area of Ogden, Utah. Under the impressive leadership of Pastor Les Magee, Washington Heights Baptist Church made Utah history by becoming the first Evangelical church to regularly attract over 1000 worshipers at its two regular Sunday services. Pastor Magee led the ministry of Washington Heights for nearly twenty years, from 1983 to 2003, and he did so by providing a missional framework in which the church operated. Having had foreign mission experience before coming to Utah, he was convinced that an Evangelical church could grow large in Utah if it sought to engage its culture with love and truth. Under Pastor Magee's direction and other like-minded Utah Evangelical churches, the Gospel began to be proclaimed in a more positive tone, not one of constant contrast to the different teaching of Mormonism.

It was not that such Utah churches and ministries compromised themselves or neglected the differences between Evangelical teachings and Mormon doctrines, but that the harsh rhetoric and negativity began to be replaced by more sensitive instruction and training. Evangelical churches began to approach the LDS community more and more in the spirit of friendship and love and less and less in the spirit of conflict and anger. Let it be acknowledged that this process and change of emphasis took a great deal of time and much effort. In fact, it continues today. Let it also be acknowledged that it was and is easy for many within the LDS community to remain suspicious and unconvinced that Evangelicals are changing their attitudes towards Mormon people in any real or genuine way.

EFFECTIVENESS

ONE CAMP WITHIN Evangelicalism embraces the more traditional form of classic apologetics: Christians are charged to proclaim the truth of Jesus Christ in the face of unorthodox teaching with clear and biblical objectivity. Such an approach often employs the techniques of debate and confrontation. The other perspective on witnessing within a Mormon culture is described more relationally as bridge-building and uses friendship and dialogue to engage with individuals whose beliefs are different. Let me be clear and upfront in admitting that I am a converted proponent of building bridges to the LDS community as a result of my years of pastoral ministry here in Utah. I have become convinced that without genuine relationship with others it is nearly impossible to have any strong influence among them. At the same time, I am fully aware of the counter-cult philosophy that if a person's house is burning down while they are asleep within, one should cry out, bang on the door, break a window or whatever might be necessary to awaken the individual who is in danger of being burned to death.

Such warnings are given as a genuine desire to love one's neighbor. As I have already admitted, however, I believe that a relational effort of genuine friendship will do more to advance the gospel in Utah than simply declaring to our Mormon friends that they are wrong and not truly Christian. I fear and have seen personally that the strict use of apologetics to help Mormons see the errors of their ways can produce a prideful and contemptuous attitude towards them that does nothing more than convince them of the truthfulness of their own faith. I believe it is easier than some would admit to let our theological concerns for others become a justification for contempt, pride, disrespect, unloving and even obnoxious attitudes towards others with whom we disagree. As apologist and philosopher Ravi Zacharias has observed, "When we throw dirt at others, two things tend to happen—we lose ground and get dirty in the process."

Mormonism has continued to grow around the world and at the time of this writing numbers about 13 million with a full-time missionary force of some 50,000+. We would have to acknowledge as well that in Utah we have not seen much of a percentage gain in the Evangelical community within the last 100 years of ministry efforts. If our goal has been to create a theological divide that clearly defines Evangelicals against Mormons and vice versa, I would say we have been quite successful. If our goal has been to convert our theological other to our way of thinking and weaken the influence of each other's movements, I would say we have not been successful at all. Evangelicalism, as a loosely employed term, is said to number some 700 million worldwide, and with all of its resources and information has not been able to slow down the growth of Mormonism around the world. The last ten years of ministry in Utah have shown us that there is a better way; the future can bring greater harmony and peace between Mormons and Evangelicals; and both communities can look to the one true God to bring us all closer to His truth than we might have ever imagined.

In recent years I have been invited to preach in a number of different Utah Evangelical churches and frequently addressed the topic, "Imagine What God Could Do If..." Each of the churches was very different: one was a Southern Baptist Church in Logan, one was a PCA Church in Layton, one was an Evangelical Free church in Roy, one was a nondenominational church in Salt Lake City, and another CMA church in Draper. The response to this message from all five congregations has convinced me anew that Evangelicals in Utah are as hopeful as ever that God is moving in our state and that good things are taking place between Latter-day Saints and Evangelicals. There is a strong and growing sentiment that Evangelicals are longing to build loving relationships with our Mormon neighbors, where, yes, we can share truth with one another, but where love and respect truly guide the way (I Peter 3:15).

In my sermon I asked: Would we suffer from what I call the *Jonah Syndrome*, where we literally become angry with God for saving people in a way that we feel is too easy or not demanding enough? Or do we long to see a day where Mormons and Evangelicals could embrace one another in true Christian fellowship? May I say again, that I wish not to be misunderstood. I am not saying this has yet happened or that enough theological concurrence exists between Evangelicals and Mormons for us to grant "Christian enough" status towards each other. Mormonism still contends that it is restored Christianity and that it alone has God's full truth and divine authority. Evangelical Christianity still contends that fundamental doctrines of Mormonism are unorthodox and inconsistent with biblical teachings. What I am asking from the pages of Jonah is, Are we ready, willing, and enthusiastic about what God might and could do in our time within our two faith communities?

If God moved among the LDS Church to adjust, discover, clarify, give new perspective or emphasis to some areas of doctrine, would the Evangelical community just dismiss and mock Mormonism and Mormon people with the accusation of superficiality and dishonesty? Would we be willing to meet out on the bridge of relationship and discuss truth and let God guide us all in a process that might be different than we might have imagined? Can we not seek understanding that we might be understood, to borrow from LDS leadership guru Stephen Covey? Can we not offer genuine love and acceptance regardless of whether we convince a Mormon friend of our truth or not? Does God not care for all of us, Evangelicals and Mormons? If He has something He wants to do in and through us and between us, are we not willing to let Him do it? As He rebuked Jonah of old, will He have to rebuke our generation, saying, "Should I not be concerned for this great people?"

A New (yet old) Approach

S OME YEARS AGO, my wife Jill and I set sail in a new ministry direction after nine years in local pastorates and formed a Utah-based mission organization that we call "Standing Together." Standing Together exists to advance Biblical unity among the Evangelical Christian community of Utah, that we might be more effective in reaching our culture with the good news of the Gospel. During the formation of our ministry and while expanding our network of Evangelical churches and pastors here in Utah, which now numbers close to one hundred relationally-based ministries, I have come to embrace some important convictions about how we Evangelicals share our faith with those we believe are not yet walking in the light.

PRINCIPLE #1: *Genuine Christian love and witness should be tangibly expressed to Latter-day Saints.* Having dedicated the last 24 years of my life to sharing the gospel with Mormon people, and having done so through a variety of methods, I am amazed at how consistently I am asked by Mormons, "Why do Evangelicals hate us so much?" If the truth of Jesus Christ as understood from an

Evangelical perspective is right, should not those with whom we seek to share it have some reason to believe that we are sharing our truth with them in love? I will never forget the evening the tenth circuit court of appeals in Denver ruled against the Mormon Church and its desire to prevent individuals from witnessing on their Main Street Plaza, a one-block section of Main Street that the LDS Church had purchased to connect Temple Square with their headquarters buildings. Viewing the local evening news that night with a University of Utah student, we were both amazed at what the TV newscast captured. An individual, thrilled with the court's decision, wanted to be among the first persons to legally pass out literature on the Main Street Plaza. The man passing out literature was being yelled at by what was obviously an angry LDS woman, who was screaming at the man, "Why do you people hate us so much?" The man, continuing in his efforts, simply responded back in kind by yelling, "We don't hate you. We love you." Surely offenses do arise when we affirm our faith commitment, but I would make the case that too many Mormon people feel that Evangelical Protestants literally disdain them as a non-Christian cult. If a person were to ask my wife, "Jill, do you feel and believe that Greg loves you?" and she were to say, "Well, I know that he tells me he does, but for the most part I don't feel very loved by him," what would the inquirer be inclined to think? I think the average person would say that our marriage is in need of some immediate counseling, and that either Jill or I or both of us need to learn how to express and receive love.

In April 2004 our ministry organized an outreach on North Temple Street during the semi-annual LDS General Conference. After two days of expressing love and kindness to Mormons on their way in and out of their meetings in their Conference Center (what we called "Mission Loving Kindness"), I was approached by an LDS security agent. He asked if he could share a few thoughts with me. He had closely observed our effort, which included some 84 individuals from seven different local Evangelical congregations. He told me that in his extended career as a security agent for the LDS Church he had seen it all, all the protest groups that had come and gone to denounce Mormons and Mormonism over the last three decades, but that what our group did was completely foreign to him. He observed that "in 34 years of service, I have never seen this." I asked him to be more specific. He went on to say, "I've never seen a group come here just to be nice to us." What a moment for the both of us, what an opportunity to consider the obvious. All I could tell this man was, "Well, I guess after 34 years, it's about time you experienced some kindness from Evangelicals."

I am not advocating an emotional, syrupy kind of Christian love that fears and avoids sharing the uncompromising message of Christ's love. What I am saying is that it is important for people whom we say we love enough to share the truth with, to sense that we really do love them and that our overriding concern is not just to prove them wrong. To reference the oft-quoted line attributed to Francis of Assisi, "Preach the gospel always and, if necessary, use words."

PRINCIPLE #2: *Building genuine friendships with Mormons is not a compromise of truth but an opportunity to share biblical truth more effectively with them.* We have all heard the line, "it's all about relationships," and when it comes to sharing spiritual truth with people this is absolutely the case. As I mentioned earlier, over the years that I have sought to engage Mormon people regarding orthodox doctrine, I have moved from the more confrontational style to value a more relational approach. In the years that I have ministered full-time in Utah, I have seen that in building genuine friendships with Mormon people I am far more effective in discussing biblical truth with them now than in my days of a more confrontational style.

Indeed, if influence is going to take place in the lives of people with whom we disagree, then we must prove that we can go the distance and maintain a loving relationship. Over the last several years I believe we have seen a paradigm shift where more and more Evangelicals are seeking to build and maintain loving relationships with Latter-day Saints, trusting the Lord for his will to be accomplished. A friend of ours who lives in Colorado shared with us the impact of our ministry in her life. She confessed that in the past whenever she saw an LDS chapel she would pray that God would open up the ground and destroy the building. After telling her how "loving" her prayer sounded, she then stated that God had changed her heart and that now she prays that God would make His love known to the Mormon people. My heart was blessed by this changed perspective, and I encouraged my friend by saying that I am sure no Mormon alive would be bothered by such a prayer.

PRINCIPLE #3: *In relationships with Mormons, seek to understand where they are spiritually; don't assume you know what they do and do not believe.* This principle has come to truly revolutionize my relationships with Latter-day Saints in the last decade. For far too long my approach to witnessing to Mormons was to arm myself with all the arguments against Mormonism, to denounce false teachings, plead with Mormons to see the contradictions in their faith, and reject it. Never mind the fact that as a young Latter-day Saint myself, I had been taught that when people accused me of not being truly Christian this only proved my faith because Satan would naturally want to persecute those in the truth. It sometimes appears to me that some Evangelicals want to persuade modern day Mormons to embrace the most obscure doctrines of Mormonism only to then rebuke them for believing such heresy. Why do we need to take up great amounts of time to convince someone that Mormonism once taught that Adam was God, for example, when they don't believe this themselves and are not going to leave Mormonism on the grounds of some doctrine that has not really been taught since the days of Brigham Young?

I would suggest that we simply ask questions of our Mormon friends and let them tell us what they believe. How many times have I heard my friend, Dr. Robert Millet, declare that he is the world's expert on what Bob Millet believes? He then expresses his shock when Evangelicals, who hear him explain his beliefs, tell him, "You can't really believe what you just said." Now, there is nothing wrong with asking honest questions about Mormonism and seeking to understand a person's particular beliefs, to be sure. I think for example, that it is very appropriate to ask a Mormon friend what his or her understanding might be of how a person is saved from their sin. If the Mormon says that it is by being good and by doing good works alone, then it is completely appropriate to ask them how they understand biblical passages that tell us we are saved by grace alone. If, however, they provide an answer to this question or others like it in a biblically accurate way, why do we have to challenge their honesty? One might say that they had not understood Mormonism to teach what the individual Mormon has claimed, and seek further clarification, but I see no need to suggest that the Mormon one is speaking with is being dishonest when asked what they believe.

PRINCIPLE #4: *More often than not, contentious labels often hinder the process of genuine spiritual dialogue.* Statements that Mormons are not true Christians, that they belong to a cult, or that they worship a false Jesus—these are classic examples of conversation stoppers, expressions that diminish the possibility that a constructive conversation will follow. Mormons are offended and hurt when we denounce their faith in such a stereotypical fashion, and why should they not be? Someone once approached me, for example, and told me I was not a true Christian because I was not baptized in the correct church. I would have you know that it was not my immediate reaction to comply with this accusation and immediately ask them to direct me to the nearest "correct church," where I could get right with God.

As Evangelicals, why then do we believe such a trivial dismissal of someone's belief system is going to produce loving and meaningful discussions about spiritual truth? I agree completely with Ken Mulholland, the former President of Salt Lake Theological Seminary, that a more appropriate statement defining Mormonism today is not that it is a "cult" but that it is a culture. The term *cult*, no matter how carefully you define the word, is clearly pejorative and only causes offense to Mormons when used to label them. Perhaps such a label makes things easier for us Evangelicals when explaining what Mormonism is to our children and teens by simply calling it a "cult," but I would counter that such a caricature is too simplistic and too dismissive. Mormons have been denounced as a cult for years and they totally understand the negative connotations of the term. If the term cult and other similar labels are a hindrance to authentic dialogue taking place between Mormons and Evangelicals, and even more disturbing, if such labels are used to be unkind and insulting to Mormons, then no wonder they reject such approaches and interactions with Evangelicals.

Stephen Robinson, a professor of religion at BYU, tells a haunting and painful story. While pursuing his doctoral degree at Duke University, he attended a community meeting of religious leaders seeking to confront the perils of pornography in their area. After a few moments, Stephen and his LDS associates were asked to leave the meeting because other religious leaders were threatening to leave if the Mormons stayed. The Latter-day Saints decided to leave the meeting rather then upset things. His final comments about this event were extremely painful to me as an Evangelical. Robinson remembers leaving that meeting realizing that some Evangelical Christians hated Mormons more than they hated pornography! Is this the message that Evangelicals want to communicate?

PRINCIPLE #5: *Latter-day Saints and Evangelicals are too prone to define their own doctrines by advancing the extreme opposite of what the other faith believes.* More and more I am convinced that this principle is a major hindrance for theological reconciliation between Mormons and Evangelicals. If Evangelicals believe we are saved by grace, then Mormons believe they are saved by works. If Mormons believe in a subjective epistemology, then Evangelicals embrace rationalistic epistemology. If Mormons are polytheists, then Evangelicals are monotheists. I do not deny in the items I just mentioned that theological differences do exist, but too often both Evangelicals and Mormons are prone to define themselves as theological opposites without engaging in serious discussion. To be honest, I believe today that both faith and reason play a role in my religious convictions and I need not feel my arguments against Mormonism are weakened because I admit such a fact. Vice versa, I need not assume that Mormons all check their brains at the doors of the wards buildings because they believe whatever they are told to believe or what they feel is true. Again, if I engage with a Mormon who makes wild theological statements and simply defends such statements as a matter of faith, it is totally appropriate to remind such a person that Isaiah reminds us to "come and reason together"—faith and reason need to come together for truth to be coherent.

This last year I was discussing the famed Christian hymn, "Amazing Grace," with an LDS general authority, and he expressed how much he appreciated the hymn. In so doing, I asked him why such a great hymn of faith would not be included in the Mormon hymnal. His answer was quick and decisive, "It's not in our hymnal for one very basic reason: we think of it as a Protestant song, but there is nothing in the hymn that any Mormon should find fault with doctrinally." He went on to say that he has instructed his wife that when he dies he wants to have that hymn sung at his funeral. I was delighted and encouraged by his honest assessment of the place of this hymn and hopeful that perhaps some day it will be sung by Latter-day Saints in the same way that Evangelicals delight in it.

To be honest, black and white conversation, argument by extremes, and labeling people are a lot easier than taking the time to listen, asking respectful questions, and pursuing truth with our friends of other faiths. But just imagine what God could do when people put aside their own agendas to let God's agenda unfold. Paul's word to the Corinthians has helped me in this regard, when he acknowledges that he had planted, Apollos had watered, but that God had given the increase (1 Corinthians 3:6). I think we Evangelicals and Mormons would do well to step back, set aside our agendas, seek truth with each other, and be determined to accept truth wherever we might find it.

CONCLUSION

To be honest and fair, there are only so many scenarios that might play out in the days to come between Evangelicals and Latter-day Saints. We can entrench ourselves in continued polemical confrontation, Mormons claiming to be the only true Christianity and rejecting all other expressions as false, Evangelicals denouncing Mormonism as a counterfeit form of Christianity and simply a cult. Or there's a second possibility: one day we might find one faith community completely embracing the other's truth and renouncing their own. In this second scenario, of course, it is far easier for each side to see the other faith community embracing their faith rather than being the one to conform. So, either things stay confrontational or Evangelicals accept Mormonism as Christian or Mormons jettison their own teachings and accept our view of historic orthodoxy. But is there no other perspective? For the purist probably not, but maybe there is something that God will do amongst us to advance His truth in a way that defies our traditional paradigms.

Might we not consider historical situations in our world where we have seen situations thought to be unchangeable totally turned upside down. Ronald Reagan led the way to a new kind of interaction between the United States and the former Soviet Union, and today our former worst enemy is now more of a friend and no longer our greatest threat. The apartheid system of South Africa is now no more, and Nelson Mandela became the first black president of that nation. In our own country, while always a problem, we are not the racist nation we once were, and things are much improved. You see, things can and do change; people and institutions do too, not always in the way we think they will, but change does happen, often in very surprising ways.

I am prone to use the illustration of the caterpillar that cocoons itself to become a butterfly. I do not know how this metamorphosis takes place; it completely baffles me: an insect without wings instinctively cocoons itself and while cocooned changes to become a flying creature. I may not be able to fathom the hows of such a rather miraculous phenomenon, but one thing I do know is that if we take some scissors, open up the cocoon before the insect transforms, it will most certainly die. In other words, in order to see what God is going to do, we just have to wait. If we did open this chamber of change what would we find? Would we discover a bizarre thing, now half caterpillar and half butterfly?

Again, if we insist on perceiving and explaining every aspect of this transformation we know as a growth unto greater religious understanding and love, we will ultimately destroy the very thing that God intends to do. Whatever takes place inside a cocoon, rest assured it is a messy process. Likewise and candidly, I do not know what God is going to do among Evangelicals and Latter-day Saints, but I pray regularly that He changes things so that both Mormons and Evangelicals will one day walk in the light in enough of a way that we are both truly following Jesus Christ sufficiently to be saved. I am simply calling upon Mormons and Evangelicals alike to look to Jesus to become all that He desires to make us and allow His transformational work to be done in all of us.

In November 2004 a coalition of Standing Together (with 50+ Utah Evangelical churches) and several educational institutions united to bring Ravi Zacharias to Utah for a three-day lectureship, which included an historic opportunity for Ravi to speak at the Mormon Tabernacle on Temple Square in downtown Salt Lake City, something that not has been done since D.L. Moody did so in 1899. Ravi's speaking engagements at the University of Utah and Weber State University were outstanding. Over and over, I was asked by people how an arrangement was secured for Ravi to speak at the Mormon Tabernacle. During a personal meeting with the LDS First Presidency, I asked President Gordon B. Hinckley directly why the LDS Church would permit such a gathering in the Tabernacle. His simple answer was that, "it sounded like a good idea, and we wanted to be helpful." Conspiracy theories aside, is it possible that God simply answered many prayers for such an event to take place where Mormons and Evangelicals could gather together in an historic Mormon location to hear one of Evangelicalism's premiere Christian philosophers preach about the uniqueness of Jesus Christ as the Way, the Truth, and the Life? As Ravi, Bob Millet, and I met personally with President Hinckley and his two counselors, I sensed that indeed God is opening up long closed doors and that a new thing, a new time of interaction was unfolding.

Can we not look to Jesus Christ, the author and finisher of all true faith, and lift up His name, knowing that when we do, He promises to draw all people to Himself? Think of the good to be gained if ever the Evangelical and Latter-day Saint relationship could be transformed by the wonderful and matchless love of God, and if together we could seek the grace of Jesus Christ, even He who knows what God can do among us. Yes, things might get a little messy along the way and some will no doubt want to "open the cocoon" before it is ready, but if we are patient, maybe, just maybe, some day Mormons and Evangelicals will be transformed by the very Savior we both profess to embrace and be able to sing together of God's amazing grace.

Appendix C

Some Guiding Principles of Constructive Conversation

1. In spite of what many people have accepted as fact, religion is an area that can be discussed and discussed seriously without dispute or confrontation.

2. One need not compromise their faith conviction in order to have a loving relationship and ongoing conversation with someone of a different religious persuasion.

3. Building relationships takes time. Some things cannot be rushed.

4. Not every doctrinal issue needs to be addressed or resolved in a single conversation.

5. Man's timetable and God's timetable may be two different things. Healthy interfaith dialogue defers to God's agenda rather than to individual or private agendas.

6. We must allow God to do His own work in the hearts of individuals. What we may desire for them to become may be very different than what God desires.

7. A good test for loving relationships is the extent to which the individual with whom we are engaged actually feels loved through the encounter.

8. There must come a point where we take the word of the individual regarding what he or she believes.

9. Building friendship is more worthwhile and fulfilling than winning an argument. Successful interfaith dialogue results not alone in winning an argument but in enhancing a friendship.

10. God is in the business of people, and so must we be. People and people's feelings matter.

11. Though labels and categories often prove beneficial, they certainly have limitations. Just because an individual belongs to a particular religious denomination does not necessarily mean that we know exactly what they believe.

12. There are risks associated with serious and sincere interfaith dialogue. Despite our best intentions, others may well misunderstand what we hope to accomplish.

13. When love and trust have been established, defensiveness is put aside and persons in dialogue can deal with most any issue, even difficult ones.

14. While theological differences exist, it is critical that we understand accurately what those differences are. Thus when we disagree, we disagree properly, over the correct issues.

15. One of the unanticipated blessings of interfaith dialogue is that one not only learns a great deal about the other person's faith but in the process also learns a great deal about their own.

16. We must not become impatient or results-driven as we engage in interfaith dialogue. The Bible

teaches us that it is God's job to change a human heart, not ours.

17. Interfaith dialogue can be helped along by a good dose of curiosity; because we live in a world of immense diversity, we simply ought to be interested in what other people believe.

18. Each person should be prepared to provide, as the Apostle Peter taught, a reason for the hope within them. This is to be done, however, with gentleness and respect (1 Peter 3:15).

19. Being prideful or judgmental rob the participants of what they might otherwise experience.

20. A healthy friendship begins to broaden well beyond religious conversation and allows for outside interaction and even social enjoyment between the parties.

21. It is more natural to want to argue and debate than to make the effort to engage in thoughtful, polite, and meaningful conversation. Loving dialogue is much more difficult to achieve than debate and argument.

22. As trust, respect, and love for another human being grows through the process of dialogue, the participants begin to feel a sense of responsibility for the other. Because one would never want to be misrepresented, he or she does all in their power to ensure that the other party's point of view is properly stated and represented.

23. As interfaith dialogues continue, a heightened sense of loyalty begins to develop, such that neither party would state privately anything that they would not make known publicly. There must be consistency and integrity between interpersonal and private expressions.

24. We need not fear healthy inter-religious conversation, because there is great richness in such a pursuit. The process proves to be both emotionally and spiritually rewarding, and one's life experiences are enhanced because of it.

25. God's ways are not our ways, and so consequently we cannot always see what He is bringing to pass.

Dr. Robert L. Millet is Professor of Religious Education, Outreach, and Interfaith Relations at Brigham Young University in Provo, Utah. Before joining the BYU Religion faculty in 1983, Professor Millet received his bachelors and masters degrees from BYU in Psychology and his Ph.D. from Florida State University in Religious Studies. Since being at BYU he has served as chair of the department of Ancient Scripture, dean of Religious Education, and Richard L. Evans Professor of Religious Understanding. He is the author of over fifty books and 150 articles, dealing mostly with the doctrine and history of the LDS Church and its relation to other faiths. He and his wife Shauna are the parents of six children and reside in Orem, Utah.

Reverend Gregory C.V. Johnson was raised in the Mormon Church but became an evangelical Christian in his mid-teens. Since graduating from Westmont College in Santa Barbara, California (1989) and Denver Theological Seminary (1992), he has served pastorates in three different Utah evangelical congregations over a nine year period. Reverend Johnson is passionate about Christian unity in Utah, and so in 2001 he left the local church pastorate to begin a missional organization called, Standing Together. His ministry vision is to advance Christian unity among evangelical congregations and pastors and to foster a culturally sensitive dialogue between evangelicals and Mormons. He and his wife Jill are the parents of four children and reside in Lehi, Utah.